DE-STRESS
YOUR LIFE
IN 7 EASY STEPS

A holistic guide to help you develop a positive mental
outlook, overcome problems and cope with the stress
and pressures of modern-day living

Glenn Harrold

I dedicate this book to Alyson Harrold
for her love, friendship and support

First published in Great Britain in 2007 by
Orion Books
an imprint of the Orion Publishing Group Ltd
Orion House, 5 Upper St Martin's Lane,
London WC2H 9EA

1 3 5 7 9 10 8 6 4 2

A CIP catalogue record for this book is available
from the British Library.

ISBN: 9780 75288 608 4

Printed in Great Britain by Clays Ltd, St Ives plc

The Orion Publishing Group's policy is to use papers that are
natural, renewable and recyclable and made from wood grown
in sustainable forests. The logging and manufacturing processes
are expected to conform to the environmental regulations of
the country of origin.

Every effort has been made to fulfil requirements with regard to
reproducing copyright material. The author and publisher will be
glad to rectify any omissions at the earliest opportunity.

www.orionbooks.co.uk

Contents

Introduction

Welcome

The aim of this book (and the attached CD) is to help you banish stress from your life and cope with the pressures of modern day living. With its holistic approach, it will also help you to create a more positive outlook and develop a stronger sense of self-worth. Modern day life can be stressful – it has been said that, in our generation, we make more decisions in a week than our grandparents made in a year. In our busy lives we are bombarded with information and often juggle many different balls in the air. Life in the twenty-first century can indeed be stressful if not checked.

The technological revolution has made life faster and changed the way we work. We want and expect so much more from life than previous generations. This is fine, but the price we sometimes pay for our busier, faster lifestyle is more stress. If you want or expect very little from life, you may avoid feeling stressed too often, but unless you choose to pack it all in, become a hermit and live in a cave, you are going to have to learn to deal with modern day stress.

In today's world we face many more pressures and dilemmas

than previous generations. We live in an increasingly commercial world where the truth is often hard to decipher. Much of the information we receive from newspapers, television and radio often comes with its own agenda. Advertising has become a very sophisticated business. As a hypnotherapist, I often notice the subliminal techniques used in some modern advertisements. It is no wonder people stress over making decisions, as very little is as it seems, but with a little knowledge, you can empower yourself and make more good decisions than bad ones, and avoid some of today's pitfalls.

Fifty years ago people had very few choices and, subsequently, fewer decisions to make. They didn't face many of the pressures that we do today and life was much more black and white. For the majority, there were minimal opportunities to improve your quality of life. However, as most working-class people were in a similar position, no one fretted too much over the status quo. They had their worries and troubles, but the pace of life was slower and stress was not a commonly used word.

However, I wouldn't want to go back to those bleak, predictable times. We live in a wonderful age with a wealth of opportunities available to almost everyone in the Western world. Even twenty or thirty years ago, it was only the well-off who travelled and holidayed abroad. Nowadays, people from all walks of life travel overseas for their holidays, often many times a year. There are millions of opportunities to create success and wealth that are available to all regardless of background. Anyone with drive, determination and a good idea can be successful. Just two or three generations ago such opportunities to progress in life were unavailable to all but a few.

The 7 steps in this book will help you to develop a more positive attitude and to face the many challenges of twenty-first century life in a natural, holistic way. When you create a strong, positive mental outlook you will be able to deal with stress and cope with the pressures that life throws at you. Creating a balance in your life is very important. As a full-time hypnotherapist, I have helped many clients who have been very successful in their careers but have neglected their health and home life. It's no good having a couple of million in the bank if your ticker gives out early because you have driven yourself too hard. You can still lead a busy and full life and yet avoid burnout by creating more balance in your life. Life is all about balance and being in tune with your mind and body will help you achieve that equilibrium.

> 'The aim of life is self-development. To realize one's nature perfectly – that is what each of us is here for.'
> **Oscar Wilde**

If you often feel overstressed, the techniques in this book and the hypnotherapy sessions on the CD will help you to feel much more in control. Stress is something that is prevalent when we close down and stop seeing the joy and abundance in life. Get into the habit of getting rid of the things that cause you to feel fear and anxiety and then fill your life with positive things instead. If you make many of the small changes suggested in this book, you will soon find that things that once caused you stress will no longer bother you. Challenge yourself regularly and live your life with courage and confidence. When you practise living like this you will be able to cope with almost anything life throws at you.

About me

For many years I worked as a musician. In my teens I played bass in a punk band that morphed into a pop band, which went on to have an all too brief taste of success in the early eighties. Later on I made a living playing covers in pubs, bars, hotels and restaurants. One of these gigs was a show in a working man's club where we shared the bill with a stage hypnotist. I had always been fascinated by the power of the mind and, after watching the show, I decided to learn hypnosis. It was a 'Eureka' moment.

I didn't want to learn hypnosis just to make people do whacky stuff. The stage show thing did not interest me at all. I was drawn to hypnosis because of its potential to heal and transform. This is the difference between stage hypnosis and hypnotherapy. The former uses hypnosis largely to entertain while the latter uses hypnosis to help and heal. Once I had made the decision to study hypnosis as a healing tool, I found the most comprehensive hypnotherapy course in the UK. After two years of hard graft and intense studying, I passed all the exams. From there I went on to build a busy private practice and gained great personal satisfaction from helping people get over all kinds of anxiety-related problems. I have treated thousands of clients in a one-to-one setting. I have dealt with every kind of stress-related problem and treated all types of phobias. I have helped people to lose weight, stop smoking, overcome fears, overcome sleep problems, and build their self-confidence and self-esteem.

After gaining this invaluable grass-roots experience, I drew upon my musical background and began making hypnosis tapes, primarily to support my work with my clients. This was another 'Eureka' moment, as the combination of my hypno-therapy experience and recording knowledge enabled me to make effective tapes. I went on to sell them in many stores, and I started my own publishing company to market and distribute them. I had no experience of marketing or publishing but simply used my self-hypnosis skills to help me succeed in business. At the time of writing, my hypnosis tapes and CDs have sold in excess of 500,000 copies worldwide and they are the UK's best-selling self-help CDs of all time. Later on in the book I will share with you many of the techniques that have helped me to achieve success.

How the book and CD work

Your imagination is a powerful tool that can help you make positive changes to the way that you deal with situations. The following story demonstrates just how powerful the human imagination can be and what can be achieved if you literally put your mind to it. The tale is about a high-ranking American POW who was incarcerated for seven years during the Vietnam War. In his prison cell he had very few privileges and was not allowed any reading or writing material. At home he had been a keen golfer and, to stay sane, he developed a daily mental visualisation technique. Every day he would lie down on his bed, relax his mind and body, and visualise himself playing a perfect round of golf. He would imagine himself playing eighteen holes, starting with the tee off at the first hole, through to putting in on the last green. He pictured the weather, the condition of the greens, tee box placement on each hole and where the flags were placed on the greens each day. He pictured the whole scene in great detail, using all of his five senses to make it realistic, and ran it like a video in his mind. He would also visualise it as though he was looking out through his own eyes and actually hitting every ball. This creative daily mental workout, as well as keeping his sanity intact, also helped him to pass the time.

When he was eventually released after seven years, an amazing thing happened. His handicap had dropped from sixteen to five. This is a monumental leap forward that would normally take years of practice. Even though he had not set foot on a golf course for years, his golf had dramatically improved simply by visualising playing the perfect round every day of his imprisonment. He was developing his golf skills in the same way as if he was actually playing. This is because of a key ingredient in mind programming – the human mind doesn't distinguish between what is real and what is imagined. So, when you create a visualisation, your mind will accept it as a reality. Studies have even shown that just by visualising exercise workouts, your body can show signs of increased conditioning and even muscle toning. Needless to say, avoiding negative imagery and regularly creating positive visualisations can help you in many different ways. We are all blessed with the ability to imagine, and when we learn how to harness the power of our imagination we can achieve practically anything.

Throughout this book there are a number of self-hypnosis techniques and visualisations that will help you use your imagination to improve many areas of your life. The book covers many of the areas that cause stress and includes lots of tips to help you deal with stressful situations and so improve your life. It has a broad approach and many of the techniques can be adapted to fit your own requirements. You may find some techniques easier to use than others, and that is fine. There are short self-hypnosis and meditation scripts at the end of each chapter that compound each step and help you to focus on specific areas. The accompanying hypnotherapy CD is a powerful aid to stress reduction. Don't worry if some techniques are new to you and they seem a little unusual. With a little practise you will soon get the hang of going into deep states of mental and physical relaxation.

> 'Imagination is
> more important
> than knowledge.'
> **Albert Einstein**

A word about hypnosis

Do not be afraid of the idea of hypnosis. When you experience it you are simply in an altered state of consciousness. Even if you believe you have never been in a hypnotic trance state before, I can assure you, you have. Being in a trance is something you have experienced naturally many times in your life. For example, just before you go to sleep each night and as you awaken in the morning. This time in between being asleep and fully awake is a trance state that everyone on the planet experiences twice a day. These morning and evening trance states are called the hypnogogic and hypnopompic states. Daydreaming is another naturally occurring trance state and something that is also familiar to all of us. So altered states of consciousness and hypnotic trance states are something you often experience. You just maybe never realised it. Now you can learn how to create those states at will to empower yourself in a multitude of different ways.

When you are in a self-induced or naturally occurring trance state you will be more receptive to accepting suggestions. This is because your unconscious mind is more open and receptive at this time. It follows that when you create these receptive states through deep mental and physical relaxation you can then work on releasing patterns of behaviour that hold you back or cause you stress and anxiety. Learning how to let go of negative conditioning, and programme the unconscious part of your mind with positive conditioning, is very empowering. It is also completely safe when you follow the guidelines set out in this book. There are many self-hypnosis, meditation and visualisation techniques in the book and on the CD to help you achieve many different goals. When you read through the scripts at the end of each step you don't need to learn them word for word, they are simply guides to help you go into deeper states of consciousness, overcome problems and create new and positive patterns of behaviour.

When you start to use the self-hypnosis techniques, don't worry if you feel you're not going deep enough into trance. Affirmations and visualisations are very effective; even in the lightest trance states they will still make a big impact on your inner thought processes. Just by closing your eyes and breathing deeply and really focusing on the affirmations as you say them, you will begin to make huge positive changes in the way you think and feel about your health and well-being.

It is important that you do your affirmations regularly, as the key to absorbing new patterns of behaviour is compounding. The more you hear and accept suggestions and affirmations the deeper they become rooted in your unconscious mind. You will then respond to those new beliefs automatically. It is like learning to drive a car. At first it is hard and you make every movement with a lot of conscious effort. But by repeating and practising the movements, this new skill sinks into your unconscious mind and you learn to change gear and drive without any conscious effort. You then have an autonomic programme that responds to each task. Learning new patterns of behaviour is very similar.

When you use any of the self-hypnosis or visualisation techniques, try not to get hung up on whether it is working or not, because with all things, practice makes perfect. Self-hypnosis is a very subtle art and not the dramatic spectacle that is often portrayed in the media. The more you use the CD and practise the techniques, the better you will get at absorbing suggestions. The key is to really put your feelings and emotions into it when you are affirming or focusing on a goal. When you do this you will strengthen and reinforce the acceptance of the suggestions and affirmations. Belief also plays a big part in reprogramming. If, when you are in trance, you affirm with absolute clarity that you are completely in control of your stress levels, then you will automatically respond to this suggestion in your everyday life. When you learn to reprogramme the way you approach problems and deal with stress, you will feel in control of your life. Stress-related illness is at an all-time high, so learning to cope with stress is very important, as the knock-on effect can be very detrimental to your health.

> 'Imagination is the beginning of creation. You imagine what you desire, you will what you imagine and at last you create what you will.'
> **George Bernard Shaw**

The CD that accompanies this book is a brand new hypnotherapy recording, created specifically to compound the book's content. Track One is a powerful hypnotherapy session that will guide you into a deep state of mental and physical relaxation. You will hear a relaxing voice and specific sound effects, created in certain keys and frequencies, guiding you into a deeply relaxed state of mental and physical relaxation. In this very receptive and relaxed state you are given a number of post-hypnotic and direct suggestions to help you free yourself of stress in all areas of your life. You will then be asked to repeat special hypnotic affirmations to help you to create a more positive outlook and develop a stronger sense of self-worth. There are also a number of background echoed affirmations, which pan from left to right in your headphones. This deeply relaxing and powerful method of delivering multiple suggestions simultaneously to the unconscious mind can facilitate positive changes very quickly. At the end of Track One you will be brought gently back to full waking consciousness with a combination of suggestion and music. There are also a number of positive subliminal suggestions, (see page 171), which are embedded in the fade out music and facilitate the overall effect.

Track Two of the CD is the first of seven short tracks that contain hypnotic affirmations relating to each of the 7 steps laid out in this book. This is ideal to dip in and out of when you want to focus on any one of the steps. The CD has been designed to compound the content of the book and so I suggest that you initially listen to the CD on a daily basis. Once you feel you are in control, you can then use it to reinforce your goals anytime you feel the need. The CD is a powerful programme in itself. When you use it with the 7 steps laid out in the book you will make quantum leaps forward in many areas of your life.

Learning = power = less stress!

Where you will be in five years' time will be as a direct result of the work you do now. By purchasing this book you have taken a big step forward. Only *you* can make the positive changes needed to improve the quality of your life. You do this by first learning techniques to help you achieve this, and then putting the things you have learnt into action. When you learn

> 'To accomplish great things, we must dream as well as act.'
> **Anatole France**

something new that will help you move forward, you become more knowledgeable. When you are knowledgeable you become empowered. The saying 'knowledge is power' is very true in the case of self-improvement. When you use the many techniques in this book designed to help you overcome difficulties and to move forward, you will begin to feel less stressed, more confident and in control of your life. You can then begin to realise your full potential. Think of it as planting positive seeds in your mind that will blossom and grow and help you to achieve your goals.

Even if some of the techniques are not new to you or are not relevant to your situation, take as much as you can from the book to help your specific needs. I have been on the self-improvement road for years, but I am always looking for new ideas and inspiration to help me move forward in my life. You should never stop learning or striving to improve your lot.

A good example of this came to me in the form of a hypnotherapy client. A few years ago I received a call from an elderly gentleman who wanted my help. He lived about sixty miles away from my nearest clinic but he had one of my tapes and was determined to see me for a one-to-one hypnotherapy session. As I recall, it took him three train journeys and about three hours to reach my clinic. When he arrived he explained that he needed help with his memory as he was studying for a degree and was having difficulty remembering everything. At first I could not believe it – this lovely old gent was eighty-three! I found his positive outlook at such an age to be a real inspiration. He'd been a commercial pilot in his younger days and, in spite of his age, he was now still very determined to move forward and improve his life.

Following the 7 steps

Each one of the 7 steps covers one of the main areas of life that cause stress. At the end of each step there is a summary that you can use to go over each of the key points in that chapter. Spend a little time at the end of each step to reinforce the techniques in your mind and consider how you can assimilate these new ideas into your lifestyle. Nothing will change just through reading – you will need to be proactive. If you need to focus more on one specific step and less on another, that's fine. Be your own best therapist and focus on the areas that are most relevant to you. If, for example, finance is your main area of stress then spend more time working on the techniques in this step. At the same time, listen regularly to the financial affirmations on Track Two of the CD.

When all is said and done, overcoming problems and achieving your goals will happen if you work hard and put the effort in. You really can achieve anything when you focus your mind, and the limits as to what you achieve will be set by your own ambition. We often say that 'you can lead a horse to water but you can't make it drink'. This is never more relevant than in self-improvement therapy. Don't get bogged down in detail. Take from this book what works for you and then use it to improve the quality of your life. Put the effort and energy in and be clear about

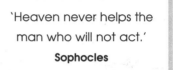

'Heaven never helps the man who will not act.'
Sophocles

your aims and you will be rewarded. Sometimes changes can be instant and dramatic, other times you will notice more gradual changes over time. In the long run, your efforts will always bear fruit.

STEP 1

De-stress and control
your stress levels

What is stress?

Stress is about feeling out of control. This feeling is often brought on by events that are not planned and cause us to feel disharmony in some way. The *Oxford English Dictionary* defines stress as 'demand on a physical or mental energy'. The very next word in the dictionary is 'stress disease', which is summarised as follows: 'disease resulting from continuous mental stress'.

Some of the mental symptoms induced by stress include anxiety, panic attacks, insomnia, fears, terrors, depression, mental fatigue, nervous exhaustion and irritability. Physical symptoms induced by stress can include tension in the body, blushing, sweating, cramp, stiff muscles, neckache, backache, tiredness and irritable bowel. Extreme, prolonged stress can lead to premature ageing, hormonal imbalances, high blood pressure, migraines, arthritis, heart problems, weight issues and more.

We know stress can lead to illness and disease, so minimising stress in your life is vitally important for your mental and physical well-being. How you cope with stress and pressure is also important. Everyone has a different stress threshold and different situations can cause stress for different people. But when you develop a more positive outlook, you will be better *equipped* to cope with stress and pressure. People with a nega-tive outlook are more prone to stress than others. We all know people who are 'born worriers', but they are usually very nega-tive people. They are the 'glass is half empty' type, as opposed to the optimist who would see

> 'If you can solve your problem, then what is the need of worrying? If you cannot solve it, then what is the use of worrying?'
> **Shantideva (8th-century Indian Buddhist)**

that glass as half full. If your mindset is positive you will not suffer with stress so much as someone with a generally negative outlook. So, developing a positive outlook is crucial and some-thing you must cultivate. The following technique will help you to feel more positive in stressful situations by detaching yourself from your negative emotions.

De-stress technique – controlling your reaction to stressful situations

- Whenever a problem or stressful situation arises, don't immediately react in a negative way. Take a few slow, deep, calming breaths and suspend your judgement.

- Imagine you are stepping out of your body and viewing the situation from above. Remain detached from any emotion or judgement.

- When you are calm and composed, take a few more deep breaths and think about how the problem can be resolved. If it is not resolvable, start to think of things you can do to improve the situation. If nothing comes to mind straightaway, affirm that your mind will find solutions when the time is right.

- Be proactive in dealing with the problem as best you can at this time.

- After dealing with the problem, imagine you are back in your body. Then ask yourself what you can learn from this situation. There is always a lesson to be learnt from every difficulty we face in life.

This positive approach will help you to keep your emotions under control when faced with difficulties. When you make this a habit, your mind and body will respond to stressful situations with more composure. In summary, avoid getting overemotional, take control of your feelings and aim to reframe problems and see them as opportunities to learn.

It can also help if you can discuss the problem with someone who has your best interests at heart – maybe a colleague, friend or partner. Other people can help you to see things differently if they have a more objective viewpoint. Discussing problems with an aim to resolve them is always a good thing.

To minimise stress in general, you need to develop a more positive approach to everything in your life. Gratitude is always a good place to start when you want to feel more positive. It is all too easy to give our attention to the things that are wrong or that don't work for us. Focus now on the things that do work for you. If you are fortunate enough to be healthy in your mind, body and spirit, take a moment to give thanks for that. If you have perfect use of your arms and legs and you have the ability to walk, run, read, write, hear, see and talk, then you are very lucky. Some people don't have these simple blessings and to have the ability to do one or more of these things would be their ultimate wish. I so admire the disabled athletes who compete in the Para Olympics. These men and women who achieve sporting excellence in spite of their disabilities show real courage and human strength in the face of adversity. They show the rest of us what can be overcome with a positive mindset.

If ever you get stuck in a negative rut or feel down about something, go out and buy the tape or CD recordings made by Christopher Reeve, the Superman actor who became paralysed in a horse-riding accident and eventually passed away in 2004. After his accident, he was paralysed from the neck down and needed a machine just to help him breathe. He fought against his adversity and, against all odds, he eventually had some mobility again. During this time he wrote books and produced recordings that documented his struggle. When you listen to his recordings and hear what being totally disabled is like, you will feel completely different about being able to walk down the road. You will see it as a huge gift. So, whenever you feel stuck in a rut, seek out books, CDs or even films that will help you to reframe things.

Never take your health and well-being for granted. When you wake up each morning, focus on all the positive things in your life, such as good relationships, friendships, your house, your work, etc. Even if these things are not perfect, it is healthy to focus on what you *have* got in your life rather than what you have not. Later on you can focus on achieving more and setting goals, but wherever you are in your life, having a good dose of gratitude will help you feel more positive.

De-stress technique – your first day on earth

- Imagine this is your first day on earth. You have just arrived here and you are looking at all the things you have in your life. You thought you had nothing but you can see that there are people who love you and you have many things in your life. You can see you live somewhere that keeps you sheltered and warm. Maybe you have the use of a car that gets you around? You have enough money to buy food and clothes. From expecting to arrive with nothing, you can see that you actually have quite a lot.

- If you often use the 'my first day' scenario, it will help you to see that you have many things in your life worth valuing, and this will help you to feel more fortunate. Close your eyes and focus now on all the good things in your life. Continue in your daily life to be thankful and feel blessed for these positives in your life.

Identifying personal stress

Throughout your life different things will cause you stress at different times. When you were younger, you would have experienced peer pressure, exam stress and various other school pressures. As an adult, you can face the pressure of providing for your family, career pressure or maybe the stresses of looking after your kids. In middle and old age, people worry more about their health. Self-esteem and poor self-image is something that can cause stress at any time in your life. Your stresses will change over the years and it is good to take stock now and again to evaluate what is causing you stress now.

Write down the main issues that are creating stress in your life right now. You can use the table opposite. Write each problem in a single sentence summarising the cause of stress. When you have written them down, take a moment to look at every aspect of these stresses from an unemotional viewpoint. Then clear your mind for a few seconds and imagine how each problem could be resolved in a positive way. Write down three possible positive solutions to each problem. Make sure that your solutions have an entirely positive outcome that benefits all concerned. Try not to involve the acquiescence of others when looking for the answers. This is about you independently finding *your own* solutions. If nothing comes to you at first, relax yourself a little more. Close your eyes, take ten very slow, deep breaths with a clear mind and then ask your creative mind to find answers. You can use the self-hypnosis guide on page 176 if you need more help in getting into the right state of mind for finding creative solutions.

Step 1 – De-stress and control your stress levels

STRESSES IN MY LIFE NOW	POSSIBLE SOLUTIONS

By engaging your creative mind to help you find solutions, you will be surprised at how you come up with new ideas that you had not previously considered. This is because your creative mind is a powerful, unlimited resource, whereas your intellectual, analytical mind has limited ability. More on this later! Once you have your solutions, be proactive and put them into practice. Take action and use them to alleviate the stresses in your life.

When focusing on personal stress, it is also important to dig deep and look for the underlying cause of any stresses, and identify the feelings it creates in you. For example, if you have had a row with someone and it has caused you stress. Focus on identifying the feeling it created in you and not just the reaction. Did it plug you into a negative feeling that you experience often? When you give it some thought and identify the causes of stress, then you can do something about it. Stress only becomes a serious problem if you do not address its root cause. If you lose your temper easily then there may be something underlying your behaviour. This is where you need to be your own therapist and get to the bottom of the problem.

Once again, write down how stressful situations make you feel inside. What emotions do they invoke? The aim of this exercise is to spend a little time self-analysing and bringing into your conscious awareness the things that trigger stress within you and the emotions that follow. Knowing where the problems lie is the starting point. Then, when you understand the causes, you can take steps to get rid of them forever and replace them with positive responses.

Step 1 – De-stress and control your stress levels

TYPICAL STRESSFUL SITUATIONS	THE FEELINGS THEY CREATE IN ME

When you look for any common emotional responses to different stresses, ask yourself, is there an underlying cause or a common theme? Maybe there is an unresolved issue from your past that is causing you to overreact and not deal with pressure and stress very well? If this is the case, there are a number of techniques to help you overcome any reoccurring negative patterns later in the book. The important thing for now is having an awareness of the causes of stress and how they make you react.

When you have identified some of the things that cause you stress and the feelings they create in you, you can use the following de-stress technique to control your physiological response to the problems.

The easy way to control stress

Breathing oxygen deeply into your lungs is a very underrated habit. We rarely consciously think about breathing, but practising deep breathing techniques can work wonders for your stress levels, particularly when you feel anxious or under pressure. The following diaphragmatic breathing technique is a good one to master – it will help you in many different situations.

De-stress technique – the breathing technique that will calm your mind, relax your physical body and help you to feel mentally alert

- Begin to breathe slowly and deeply in through your nose and out through your mouth in a steady circular rhythm.

If you can, close your eyes, but this is not essential. Think of nothing but your breathing. Focus on drawing the pure air into your lungs and breathing away any stale air.

- Continue this slow, rhythmical breathing and, as you inhale, push your stomach out so that you breathe into your stomach, which then expands with your in-breath. Then, as you exhale, your stomach goes in and your chest slightly expands. Practise this breathing cycle for a while until it comes naturally.

- Once you have the hang of diaphragmatic breathing, you can add on the following to the technique. Continue with your diaphragmatic breathing and make each in-breath last as long as possible so that you fill all of your lungs. Then, when you lungs are full, at the top of your breath hold it for three seconds. One, two, three. Then exhale very slowly and count to five as you do so. Continue with this pattern, keeping your breathing slow and steady. You will soon begin to feel physically relaxed and mentally calm.

This diaphragmatic breathing technique has many uses. You can use it just to calm your mind or to think more clearly. Or you may want to use it to help you solve problems. For example, think of something that stresses you. It can be any-thing, maybe a financial stress or an ongoing feud with some-one. Now, as you focus on the thing that stresses you, begin the breathing technique. Think about the problem as you go through the technique. Continue for a few minutes while focusing on the problem and also the feeling it creates with-in you. Are you holding any stress or tension in your body?

If so, begin to let it go. With every out-breath, let go of any negative feeling that arises. Just breathe it away and let the stress go. Take a few minutes to do this and make sure you release all negative feeling and tension in your body.

You will notice that by breathing in this way any stress begins to disappear and does not affect you in the same way. This can mean that your chest is no longer tight, or your heartbeat does not race anymore, or your blood pressure goes back to normal. By calming your mind in this way you will also allow your creative thoughts to surface and you may find solutions to problems. This technique will also help you to release anger and control your emotions. Slow, deep breathing is an instant way of calming the mind and body. When you breathe in this way you will draw more oxygen into your body and up to your brain, helping you to feel both mentally focused and physically relaxed. Being both alert and relaxed at the same time will help you achieve peak performance states. It is also an ideal starting point for a hypnotic induction and something many hypnotherapists use to prepare their clients for going into deeper states of relaxation.

The beauty of this simple technique is that you can use it anytime you like to compose yourself and keep your stress levels down. If you get into a dispute, or something happens to cause you stress, use this breathing exercise to take control of your stress levels. Similarly, if you have an important meeting or need to make a speech or give a performance of some kind, slow, deep breathing with a positive focus will help you to create a peak performance state in which you are relaxed and yet alert and focused. There is more on creating peak performance states later.

Reframing stress and pressure

Feeling frustration or disappointment within yourself can cause stress. If you feel you have failed at something, or not achieved what you want, it is natural to feel disappointed. If you allow that frustration to go inward and you give yourself a hard time, it can cause a lot of personal stress. Many people, particularly men, don't talk about their failings, as they don't like to let others know when they feel they have let themselves, or someone else, down. Feeling down is something everyone experiences from time to time. But you must never dwell on your misgivings as life is not perfect and neither are we. The key is not to allow mistakes to hold you back or become an inward source of stress. Never beat yourself up over making mistakes. Learning to accept your failures is as important as acknowledging your successes.

> 'Freedom is not worth having if it does not include the freedom to make mistakes.'
> **Mahatma Gandhi**

De-stress technique – banish negative
self-talk forever

■   This is a simple but very important lesson. Never ever speak negatively to yourself. This can be so destructive. If you repeat something often enough, your unconscious mind will soon accept it as a reality! So, if you often berate yourself by calling yourself stupid or useless, you are actually programming yourself in a very negative way. You will then unconsciously respond to that negative programming and create situations that make you feel stupid or useless.

- Think of your mind as a computer – what you put in will come back out. The human mind is exactly like that, so from now on you must NEVER vocally or internally say or even think negative things about yourself. I know this is not always easy if you have had a lifetime of negative conditioning and your self-esteem is low, but you need to start afresh from this moment on. By programming your computer with positive beliefs about yourself, you will build more confidence and self-esteem over time. So it is a case of 'fake it until you make it'. Make a habit of saying positive things to yourself, even when you mess up! If, for example, you make a mistake, detach yourself from the situation and look for the lesson in it (use the De-Stress Technique on page 18), but do not be self-critical. Even the most successful people make mistakes and errors of judgement. However, a successful person would not dwell upon their mistakes; they would learn from their error and move on. From now on view your mistakes and errors as things that will teach you something. Look for the lesson in the error but do not punish or berate yourself. Sometimes we learn the biggest lessons through our mistakes. The key is to learn the lesson so you don't make the same mistake again and retain your self-belief by maintaining a positive internal dialogue. There is more about positive programming and affirming later.

While I believe some people are naturally more adept at coping with stress and pressure than others, you can learn to cope with bigger pressures by using self-hypnosis and visualisation techniques that help to develop a more positive outlook. It takes a little effort but it can easily be done when you know how. If you can learn to roll with the punches and see problems in life as challenges, you reframe those problems and eliminate the stress of them. No one goes through life without making mistakes, but ask yourself this question: are you the kind of person who beats yourself up for making mistakes, or do you see your bad decisions as lessons that will help you to grow and become wiser?

> 'Nothing can stop the man with the right mental attitude from achieving his goal; nothing on earth can help the man with the wrong mental attitude'
> **Thomas Jefferson**

I've made countless mistakes in my life and when I was younger, I would often berate myself for being foolish. Nowadays I reframe the way I feel about making mistakes. I have learnt to accept that it is human to err, and I see my errors of judgement as part of the process of learning about life. Each of us is on our own unique journey through life and we are learning new lessons every day. If you can accept this simple understanding and reframe the way you feel about some of your failings, it will eliminate a lot of stress in your life. If you stop worrying about making mistakes or failing, you will not be afraid of taking on new challenges. Don't let fear prevent you from living your life to the full.

From now on accept that all the good and bad things you experience are life lessons. Facing challenges and overcoming difficulties instead of backing away in fear, allows you to grow and learn about life. As we get older it is easy to stop taking risks and to stay well within the comfort zone; I know of a number of people who travelled the world during their younger years with minimal resources, but some of them are now afraid to get on a plane. It is strange how this sometimes happens to people as they age. They lose their spirit of adventure and

> 'Twenty years from now you will be more disappointed by the things that you didn't do than by the ones you did do. So throw off the bowlines. Sail away from the safe harbour. Catch the trade winds in your sails. Explore. Dream. Discover.'
>
> **Mark Twain**

become afraid of taking risks. Maybe they feel they have more to lose in their later years or they become more aware of potential dangers.

The daily repetition of watching the news and reading newspapers can instil fear in people, as most news is negative. Many people ritualistically watch the news and read newspapers every day of their lives, but the repetition of this over a period of time can have a negative effect on the mind. You can still keep up-to-date with the news from the internet and be more selective about what you read. Being aware of how the mind responds to negative input, I generally avoid newspapers and try to be selective about the TV I watch. If you are a news addict, try going for a week only listening to brief headlines and see if you feel more positive by the end of the week. Also, when you feel anxious or down, minimise any outside negative influence. At these times read or watch something uplifting and empower yourself with regular self-hypnosis.

Becoming cosseted and getting stuck in dull routines can also be a cause of stress. If this is the case then you need to step out of your comfort zone and take the odd risk now and again. I did a parachute jump a few years ago for that very reason, and although the thought of it was a little scary, I never felt more alive than when I was floating down to earth watching the world go by. I'm not advocating you join the local dangerous sports club but if you are feeling stuck, take action. Do something a bit different that gets your heart going. When you challenge yourself you will feel more alive and happier.

De-stress technique – challenge yourself

- Every so often, do something new that is a little outside your comfort zone. Take on a new activity or challenge, even if it seems a little scary. In fact, scary is good, as any challenge that gets your adrenalin going will help you become very focused. New challenges will help to raise your confidence and bring out the best in you. You will also feel great afterwards and really proud of yourself.

- When you take on a new challenge, visualise it beforehand in a 100 per cent positive light. Close your eyes and relax your mind and body through deep breathing. Then imagine a video of the whole event running from start to finish and see it being a very positive experience. Make this video big and bright and very clear in your mind. If it seems scary, just breathe away any fear or trepidation. Visualise it every day in the run up to the event and you will feel fantastic when you do it for real.

- Some suggestions for challenges could be: a parachute jump, a firewalk, a glasswalk, a bungee jump, hang-gliding, public speaking, abseiling, skiing, running marathons, gliding, mountaineering, trekking, canoeing, diving, water-skiing, horse-riding.

■ Maybe combine a challenge with raising money for charity, as this will give you added motivation to succeed. But always remember when you embark upon a new challenge to run the visualisation technique at least once a day in the days leading up to the event. It will give you a good idea of how to approach the challenge and mentally prepare you in the best possible way.

Balancing your lifestyle

I lead a busier life than ever. I am constantly writing and producing audio CDs, books and DVDs. I publish many of these products through my own publishing companies and I employ over a dozen or so people. I also produce CDs for the BBC and write books for Orion. Some days I make so many decisions that my head spins. But I balance this full-on career with regular exercise, meditation, yoga, tennis and other activities that combat this potentially stressful lifestyle. I can honestly say I have very little stress in my life, in spite of it being a little fast and furious at times. For me, stress was living at the top floor of a council tower block in a poor area and struggling to pay the bills. This was a reality for me a few years ago, so I know how tough life can be for some. As they say, it is tough at the top but a lot tougher at the bottom. I speak from experience!

If you live a busy life and have many demands on your time and energy, make sure you do other activities that balance out your lifestyle. Think of the analogy of the stress bucket. When you have several stressful things going on, your bucket will gradually fill up over time and eventually overflow. This means your stress levels are out of control and will cause major problems. It can be one final little thing that pushes you over the edge and causes you to blow a fuse, lose your temper, or worse, become ill. It is not the final stressful event you are reacting to but the build up of accumulated stress. When you practise relaxation, play a sport, meditate or such like, you will be regularly emptying your stress bucket and preventing it from overflowing.

On page 116 there are some exercise motivation suggestions that will give you ideas for new, healthy activities. Work out a schedule where you incorporate one or more healthy activity into your week so that you offset your workload with plenty of play or relaxation time. If you work for forty hours or more in a week, make sure you exercise for at least fifteen minutes each day. If time is a problem, cut right back on watching TV or reading newspapers or any other idle pursuit that doesn't serve you well. You need a little discipline to get this work/play balance right, but once you do so, the healthy pursuits will become an integral part of your week. If you are top heavy with work then push yourself to find new hobbies or activities that will alleviate stress. These activities will counterbalance the pressures and stresses you face elsewhere.

Mind-clearing meditation

The following is a useful meditation technique to help you to relax your mind. It is a good way to familiarise yourself with going into a self-induced trance state. Having a clear mind is one of the best ways to combat stress and it will also help you deal with new stresses that may arise in your life. When you have a lot going on and feel mentally stressed, the following technique will work wonders in calming your mind and alleviating stress. If you are constantly going over problems in your mind, your thinking and judgement becomes clouded. But when you meditate you allow your mind to rest and recuperate. You can use this technique for twenty or thirty minutes at a time. You will be amazed at how good you will feel afterwards. You will find that you have a new perspective on problems and can deal with things with greater clarity.

> *Stop at this point and read the script through a few times until you know what to do and then practise this technique for the next few days. You will find that the more you practise, the deeper into trance you will go each time, and the better you will get at de-stressing your mind.*

- Go to a quiet room where there are no distractions. Light a candle and place it in front of you. Turn off all lights so the only light is from the flame of the candle.

- Sit comfortably in front of the candle and focus on the flickering flame. Watch the movement of the flame and begin to breathe very slowly and deeply in through your nose and out through your mouth. Make each circular breath long and deep, and clear away any thoughts so your mind becomes still and centred. Don't worry if you get the odd unwanted thought. Just centre your mind again and allow the thought to drift away. Focus on your breathing and the stillness of the moment.

- Keep your eyes on the flame and remain centred and focused. Be in the here and now and accept everything as it is. Continue with your slow, deep breathing and allow yourself to relax deeply. You can stay in this pleasant state for as long as you like. Ten-, twenty- or thirty-minute sessions are ideal. Whatever suits you at the time.

- The first time you practise this mental workout focus on nothing but clearing your mind and staying centred. Don't underestimate the power in the simplicity of this, as it can be a very good discipline for completely de-stressing your mind. Once you have practised this technique a few times and you get to the point where your mind is calm, you may decide to focus on solving a problem or letting go of a particular stress. When you do this, focus on one thing at a time and keep it simple.

- When you have finished, blow out the candle, close your eyes and notice the thoughts that come to you at this time. You will feel refreshed and relaxed and you may find you get some inspiration or that new, creative ideas may come to you.

- It is also helpful to use this meditation before you go to sleep, as it will relax you and clear your head.

Summary

What is stress? – *Understanding stress and how it may relate to you.*

Identifying your personal stress – *looking at areas of your life that cause you to feel stressed. Identifying patterns of behaviour, unearthing the causes of stress and changing how you react to stress.*

The easy way to control stress – *a stress-busting deep breathing technique you can use whenever you need to feel in control in a pressured or stressful situation.*

Reframing stress and pressure – *changing the way you view stress and learning to take on new challenges with a more positive outlook. Having more courage and self-belief will help you cope with stress in a better way.*

Balancing your lifestyle – *finding new de-stressing activities that will help you to get your work, rest and play balance in the right proportions.*

Mind-clearing meditation – *a meditation technique to learn and practise. When practised regularly it will strengthen your ability to feel mentally calm and give you more clarity and better judgement.*

STEP 2

De-stress your finances and overcome work stress

Coping with financial stress

One of the biggest causes of anxiety is financial problems. People who are broke worry about not having enough to pay bills, and people with money have the worry of investing it prudently and finding ways to keep it from the taxman – legally of course! Worrying about money can be a big source of stress. When you worry or obsess about money you create a negativity around it that blocks you enjoying it. I know several millionaires who are as miserable as sin and just don't know how to enjoy their wealth. Most people believe that having a lot of money would solve all their problems. But how many times have we read about a lottery winner who ends up saying that the win destroyed their life? However, it is not the win that messes up their life, but their attitude to the money and their inability to cope with their instant wealth.

Whether you are rich or poor, you have to learn to develop a relaxed and positive attitude towards money. Even if you live in a crumbling tower block, as I once did, don't buy into the 'poor me' syndrome. With a little desire and determination you can always improve the quality of your life. There are millions of cheap self-help books and CDs on this topic that can help you change your circumstances and create abundance. If you want more money, that is something you can achieve if you want it badly enough. But don't fret about not having it, as you will block your natural abundance and create unnecessary stress. Yearning for, and wishing for, more money is a waste of energy. Instead you have to be clear in your aims and take action.

With credit so readily available to all it is so easy to get into debt these days, but debt is debilitating and will cause you much stress. What is the point in having a fancy car if making the monthly repayments stresses you out? Over-borrowing for luxury items is pure ego-driven behaviour that will end in tears. I have been broke and up to my eyes in debt, borrowing from Peter to pay Paul. I vowed after my debt years that I would never borrow money again other than to buy property. I hated the feeling of being constricted because I owed money. It was a huge stress for me at the time, but I learned some good lessons from it. Whatever your financial situation, always live within your means and never get greedy or allow money to corrupt you. It is only money after all!

If you are in debt or spending too much

If you are in debt, spending too much or you buy things unnecessarily, you need to get rid of this type of behaviour. Look into the reasons for any patterns of behaviour like this. Is the desire to overspend driven by something in your past? Are you trying to keep up with others by having the latest hip must-have item? Are you feeling down and trying to make yourself feel better? Do a little self-analysis here if budgeting is a problem for you. Once you get to the bottom of what drives you to overspend then you can change the behaviour. If you are trying to make yourself feel better, instead of heading off to the shops with your credit card, go for a walk in nature. Or maybe get into the habit of going swimming instead of shopping. The after-effects

> 'Annual income twenty pounds, annual expenditure nineteen six, result happiness. Annual income twenty pounds, annual expenditure twenty pound ought and six, result misery.'
> **Charles Dickens**

of exercise will always make you feel so much better than going further into debt. I know it is easier said than done, but as I have said before, this is a holistic journey and all these little steps will help you to create a happier and less stressed lifestyle. You must aim to get your fix from doing things that are good for you and not detrimental to your well-being. Debt is debilitating and reckless spending will cause you lots of grief in the long run, so you need to create strategies to help you get rid of any destructive habits regarding money.

The reason money causes people so much stress is because money is related to security, and most people strive to create security all their lives. But in this day and age, security is like the Holy Grail. It is difficult to find in a world that is increasingly insecure. Stocks and shares rise and fall like never before. Banks and big conglomerates go bust overnight. Our governments have become completely untrustworthy. Pension funds can offer little security. House price forecasts are unpredictable. Oil prices spiral ever higher. On top of all that, our daily newspapers often report many of these events with sensational

and frightening headlines, so
it is natural that people worry
and feel insecure.

Security is difficult to find
in the modern world, but
instead of worrying about all
the negatives, it can be quite

> 'It is not the strongest of
> the species who survive,
> not the most intelligent,
> but those who are the
> most adaptive to change.'
> **Charles Darwin**

liberating to accept that the world you live in is insecure, and
that change is the only certainty.

De-stress technique – embracing change

- Learning to adapt to changes will help you deal with
  many of the stresses of the fast pace of modern life. Begin
  to breathe slowly and deeply in through your nose and
  out through your mouth in a rhythmical breathing pattern.
  Close your eyes and focus on your breathing. Allow your
  mind to become clear. Take a few moments to get into a
  relaxed state.

- Now affirm to yourself that you embrace change and
  that you accept new challenges as opportunities to
  learn. Repeat this affirmation a few times: 'I embrace
  change easily'. Affirm it with real feeling and belief, and
  repeat it over and over like a mantra. When you feel
  this new belief is part of you, slowly open your eyes and
  come back to full alertness. Practise this regularly if
  change stresses you.

Our world is changing faster than ever before. In the last 100
years, life has changed more than at any other time in history,

so naturally this fast-paced and changing world makes people feel insecure. But if you learn to go with the flow of life and don't buy into fear so easily, life becomes easier. When you move forward and stay positive and creative, you will feel more personal security in spite of what is going on in the world. You won't buy into any collective fear that is often exacerbated by hysterical newspaper headlines.

7 mini steps to get out of debt, release stress about money and become prosperous

Step 1. The first and most important rule is to make sure your income exceeds your outgoings. I know that is obvious, but if you are struggling with debt, this must be your starting point. If you are in debt, you absolutely must pull your horns in and get back to basics. You need to start over again and create a good, uncluttered platform to generate more abundance in your life. On a piece of paper, write down two lists, one detailing your total monthly income and the other listing all your monthly outgoings. Look at new ways to make sure your income exceeds your outgoings. Don't fret if you have to make cutbacks – look at this as a temporary situation. It is okay to live minimalistically and to strip back to bare essentials for a while. It will serve you well and help you to really appreciate money in the future when you have more of it. This is your starting point.

Step 2. After cutting back as much as you can, work on paying off all debts. Debt is debilitating and will only stunt your journey to prosperity, so avoid it at all costs. The most important things you should spend your money on are: somewhere to live, food and clothing, household bills and maybe a vehicle, if it helps to get you to work. If you are in debt then everything else should be viewed as a luxury. So stick to only buying essentials for now, until your circumstances change. Work out a plan with your debtors to pay them off by a certain date. Stick to the plan and do not borrow any more money. If you find this difficult and are still using your credit card for non-essential items, you could cut up the card or give it to a trusted family member or friend with strict instructions not to let you have it back!

Step 3. The next rule is to let go of any worry or stress about financial matters. As mentioned earlier, by replacing reckless spending with more healthy pursuits that prevent you from getting into debt, you will begin to feel more relaxed about money. You must also avoid talking about your finances in a negative way, even if you don't have much. If you are always saying you are broke or worrying about not having enough, then this will become a self-fulfilling mantra. Instead, accept that you don't have much now (if this is the case), but do not worry about it. Think of the lean times as a short interlude in your abundant life journey. Accept the financial hiatus as it is for now and believe that abundance will soon come to you freely and naturally. The following steps will help you to achieve more prosperity, but first you must get your spending under control so that you can develop a more relaxed attitude towards money and finances.

Step 4. Once you have your finances under control and you no longer stress over lack of money, then and only then can you start focusing on creating more wealth. You now have the ideal platform to create abundance. Firstly, you need to focus on what you actually want. If you want to become rich, believe this is going to be your reality. You have to believe it will happen to you. If you just want a little more then that is also fine, just be clear about what you actually want from life in financial terms. Write down on a piece of paper the financial goals that you want to achieve and include a time frame. On page 150 there is a section called 'Setting goals for your future'. This section may help give you a few ideas to crystallize what you want to achieve. Write a list of financial goals and aims that you will achieve in both the short and long term.

Step 5. You need to create a clear belief that life is going to change for the better and that you are going to realise your goals. Read your goals every day and recite the following affirmations on a daily basis. These affirmations are very powerful when you affirm them regularly. By compounding the affirmations every day you will create a strong, new, inner belief and your financial circumstances will go from strength to strength. When you recite the affirmations, believe they are a reality *now*. Belief is very

powerful and something all successful people have in abundance.
Get into the habit of silently affirming the following phrases when you
awaken, when you shower, when
you are driving or anytime throughout the day when you have some

> 'Many of life's failures
> are people who did
> not realise how close
> they were to success
> when they gave up.'
> **Thomas Edison**

spare time. The magic words you must regularly affirm are
as follows:

* I deserve to be abundant and prosperous
* I am always in the right place at the right time
* Abundance flows freely and naturally to me
* All of my needs are constantly met

This should be your new mantra.

Step 6. Once you have created the belief, you need to
take positive action. Be proactive; put yourself in the marketplace where you can attract more money into your life.
If you are already in a full-time job, maybe start a little side-
line that has big potential. Always think big when starting
new ventures, but start small and test your marketplace
first. Only invest or borrow at this point if you have tested
the market and you know that there is genuine potential
in your venture. Don't get caught up in the fantasy – 'if this
works it will solve all my problems'. Hoping, yearning or
wishing is weak and not based in reality. It is ego-driven
and not helpful to you in the least. Don't waste your time
and energy on pipe dreams. Be pragmatic and clear-
thinking, and only speculate to accumulate if you really

feel you are onto a winner. When you are clear and decisive, others will respond to you positively.

If working for yourself is not an option, apply for new jobs that will suit your lifestyle aims and will fulfil your financial ambitions. If you feel you are under-qualified, make a plan to achieve the qualifications you need to give you the new career and financial position you are aiming for. Every successful person will have made sacrifices in their life. Sometimes you have to take one step back in life to take two steps forward. Look upon a step back, or any sacrifices, as part of your journey towards success. The journey to real, lasting abundance must be holistic.

Step 7. You need to believe that everything will come good by accepting that you deserve all the good life has to offer. You absolutely deserve to be abundant and successful. When you believe this on a deep, unconscious level, you are sending out a powerful statement of intent. With this type of unconscious programme you will find doors will open for you and you will attract into your life just what you need to become more abundant.

> 'The greatest danger for most of us is not that our aim is too high and we miss it, but that it is too low and we reach it.'
> **Michelangelo**

Follow the 7 mini steps in order and use the prosperity visualisation technique on page 59. You will soon be out of debt and on the fast track to a more financially prosperous lifestyle.

Coping with work stress

If you suffer from work stress, the important thing to do is make changes. Don't think you have to stay stuck in a rut – there are always other options. If you work in an environment that stresses you and changing jobs is not an option, look at what you can do to improve things. If your workload is excessive, it is important to be organised so that you prioritise the most important work. If you have the option, delegate the less important work. If you work long hours each week, try to balance this out with some rest and relaxation. Ensure you take a break at lunchtime; a twenty-minute self-hypnosis session in the middle of your day will help you to recharge and to be more effective. This is because when you go into a state of mental and physical relaxation, your brainwaves will slow down from the beta to alpha state and beyond. This allows every cell in your mind and body to recharge and rejuvenate. When you come back to full waking consciousness from a twenty-minute relaxation, you will feel as though you have had a long, refreshing sleep. Even if you relax for a few minutes, you will still notice the benefits. Try it for yourself. If you are in a busy office, find a quiet place in your break time where you won't be disturbed and practise the following technique.

De-stress technique – supercharging your day

- Allow yourself to get in a comfortable sitting or lying position. If you are sitting, sit upright with your feet flat on the floor and your hands flat on your thighs. Close your eyes and begin to breathe very slowly and deeply in through your nose and out through your mouth. Make each circular breath long and deep, and continue this relaxing rhythm. Breathe away any tension in your body with every outbreath.

- The important thing is to clear away any thoughts so your mind becomes still and centred. This can be a challenge if you have had a busy day or there is noise around you. If that is the case, affirm to yourself that any outside noise will fade into the background and will help you to relax even more. Remember, when you state this as a fact your unconscious mind will accept it. Don't worry if you get the odd unwanted thought. Just centre your mind again and allow the thought to drift away. Focus on your slow, deep breathing and staying centred. Even if there are loud distractions, let them fade away so they do not bother you and allow yourself to become that little bit more deeply relaxed by stilling your mind.

- If you want to simply relax and recharge, stay in this relaxed state for twenty minutes and then allow yourself to come back to full waking consciousness. Or you can use this time to connect with your creativity to find a solution to a problem. When you are in a deeply relaxed state ask yourself to find solutions to the problem. Don't intellectualise it, or think about the problem itself, just ask your mind for the solution. If suitable, visualise a positive outcome to the problem. Keep it simple as you are communicating with a different part of your self, which requires clear, direct communication. Simply state that your creative mind will come up with the right solution at the right time, and then switch off from it.

You will find you are able to work much more effectively after this brief re-charge. You may also feel more inspired in your work as you have connected with your creative mind. You can use this technique not just in an office environment, but at any time you need a boost. If you find it difficult relaxing yourself in a busy environment, use the CD in this book to supercharge. If Track One is too long, use one or more of the short booster tracks on Track Two. If there is nowhere to relax, leave the office and go for a walk. Exercise will always reduce your stress level.

If you are having problems with a colleague or boss in the workplace and you need to confront them, request a meeting to air your opinion. Before the meeting, use the self-hypnosis technique above or the more detailed one on page 176 to create a trance state so that you can visualise a positive out-come. When you visualise the meeting, imagine yourself in the room with your colleagues and see the meeting going exactly how you want it to go. See yourself getting your point of view across clearly, negotiating effectively and communi-cating your needs exceptionally well. Make the visualisation very clear, using all of your senses, see the colours and notice the aroma in the room. Make everything big and bright in your mind's eye and run it through like a video from start to finish. See yourself at the end of the meeting feeling very satisfied with the way that you expressed yourself. If you do this a few times before the actual meeting you will be amazed at how well you are able to negotiate when the time comes for real. This self-hypnosis technique works wonders in preparing you for interviews or pressure situations where you need to be at your best.

There are other ways to make your workspace less stressful. If it is possible, playing the right type of music can create a more relaxed or positive atmosphere. Calming, relaxation music is very conducive to creating a relaxing environment. Soothing music is something many relaxation therapists use to create an atmosphere of calm in their office. It also helps to change their client's state so they are more receptive to the therapy. If your office is open-plan and you can't play music out loud, perhaps you could use a personal CD player or iPod to play music that will help you to feel more relaxed. If this is not possible, just make sure that you spend your lunchtime away from your workplace or desk.

De-stress tip – using music to increase creativity and enhance learning

- If you need to concentrate and focus, Baroque music, such as Vivaldi's *Four Seasons*, can help you create an ideal state for absorbing information. Playing this music has been scientifically proven to create optimum learning states. This is because the high frequencies in the music help to stimulate certain cognitive brain functions. There have been a number of studies that prove that playing Baroque music to children before exams has significantly improved their grades. Conversely, low frequency rock music has the opposite effect.

- When you are working and need inspiration, Mozart's music is great for stimulating creativity. Again this is because of the frequency of the music. The busy patterns of Mozart's music stimulate creative brain functions and can help to alleviate anxiety and can even heal some psychological problems. It has also been discovered that the keys that music is written in can play a part in creating certain physiological states. For example, the key of G (194.71 Hz) resonates with the frequency of the earth and the colour orange-red, and has a dynamic, stimulating, and energizing effect on the mind and body. I write music in certain keys which I then use on my hypnosis CDs to further induce positive states. Using the right music in your work and home life to help you study, learn and be more creative is another little habit you should incorporate into your life.

Sound vibration has actually been proven to change the molecular structure of water. There is an excellent book on this subject called *Messages from Water* (see page 181). The author uses experiments to prove that human vibrational energy, thoughts, words, ideas and music affect the molecular structure of water. It shows that soothing relaxation music and positive words create beautiful

> 'Pleasure in the job puts perfection in the work.'
> **Aristotle**

crystalline patterns in the molecular structure of water. It also found that negative words created ugly patterns in the water molecules. When you think that our physical bodies are made up of over 70 per cent water, it becomes easy to see how music can affect our physiological and mental states. This again is why negative self-talk is something you should permanently avoid. If you want to know more about the benefits of music therapy, there is a list of references on page 182.

If you need to change the atmosphere of your workplace, there are a number of other things you can do. If it is possible, burning relaxation or uplifting oils in an oil burner can help. Lavender oil will help create a relaxing atmosphere, while ylang ylang oil is great for energising. Whatever state you want to create, there will be an aromatherapy oil to help you achieve it. Oil burning, combined with the right music, is a powerful combination as you are using multiple senses, in this case smell and sound, to achieve a certain state. If burning oils is not acceptable in your office, an alternative would be a spray bottle containing essential oils and water.

If you can make your workspace more aesthetically pleasing by de-cluttering and adding fresh plants, you will also be stimulating your sense of smell and your visual sense. Plants generate more oxygen in the atmosphere and are ideal for combating the negative ions generated by computers and other sources of radiation. Use rose quartz crystals to negate the detrimental effects of electro-magnetic fields around electrical devices. In our office we have the lot: crystals by the computers, relaxation music on the go, relaxing oils burning, and we often make time for short relaxation sessions to re-charge. For a busy publishing company, it is a surprisingly relaxed atmosphere. When you add each little step together, these small steps can become a powerful holistic force in combating a stressful work space.

If you work with people who cause you stress, this can be a tricky one as they are probably unavoidable. We can't always choose who we work with and so it can be frustrating to spend forty hours a week with someone who is an energy drain. If you work with people that cause you stress, you will need to change the way you deal with them. This means not allowing them to affect you in a negative way. The following technique will help you do just that.

De-stress technique – protecting yourself from negative or stressful people

- Close your eyes and take a few slow, deep breaths. Allow yourself to become very calm and take a moment to clear your mind. Now imagine you are surrounded by a white, protective light. Visualise a protective energy field all around your body, as though you have stepped inside a white bubble of pure, healing light.

- When you imagine this light around you, you will feel completely safe and secure. No negative energy can pass through this protective shield. If anyone criticises you or is acting negatively towards you, it will bounce off your protective shield and have no effect on you. Only positive thoughts and energy can pass through your protective light. Whenever you are around stressful people at work, use this visualisation.

- Any time you imagine you are inside this white bubble in your everyday life, you will immediately feel protected from the negative energy of others. The next time a stressy work colleague is near and you imagine you are inside your protective white light energy field, you will feel completely different. They will no longer affect you in a negative way. You will feel completely different towards them and much more in control of your feelings. You can use this technique to protect yourself from anyone who emits negative energy.

Being clear about your future

Being successful in career and money terms can mean different things to different people. For some, having a steady job with a regular income can be enough to make them feel secure and happy. Others are happy when they drive themselves to achieve big goals and thrive on new challenges all the time. Think about what floats your boat and what you really want from life. Be clear about what you want to achieve, both financially and in your work. Having goals to aim for is crucial for creating a positive outlook. If you don't have ambitions, life happens to you rather than you going out and creating your reality. You don't have to be gung-ho, just be clear about what you want life to deliver to you. Write down the things you want to achieve in your work life and the financial security that it entails.

Whenever you write down your goals and affirmations, always state them in the present tense as though they are a reality now. The aim is to prompt your mind to take ownership of the goals by stating them as a reality. Even though they may not be a reality now, you are simply programming your mind to believe they are. You must also repeat your affirmations regularly. The more you hear them, the deeper they go and stronger they become. Your unconscious mind will then accept them as a truth and you will respond accordingly.

Here are some examples:

I have a secure job with a big company working as a

_____

I earn a big salary working as a self-employed

_____

I have my own successful _____ **business**

Write your career goals below:

_____

_____

_____

_____

If you are ambitious, don't put a limitation on your goals. To pinch a quote from my book _Create Wealth and Abundance_ – shoot for the stars and you might reach the moon! Always be very specific when you affirm because your unconscious mind will interpret your phrases exactly as you state them. For example, _don't_ say, 'I am going to come into money', as the unconscious won't interpret this very well. For instance, it is possible to come into money by having an accident and receiving compensation.

The following visualisation will help you focus on achieving your work and financial goals. It will also negate any stress you have in this area.

Prosperity visualisation technique

To create the success you want in life you need to be crystal clear about your aims on both a conscious and unconscious level. The following visualisation will help you create a strong unconscious belief that you are going to achieve your aims.

> *Stop at this point and read the following script through a few times and then practise this technique as often as you wish. Your mind will soon absorb this visualisation and begin to accept it as a reality. Once the new belief is absorbed by your unconscious mind, you will respond to it automatically in your daily life. This may manifest in you, consciously or unconsciously, by creating situations and opportunities that help you achieve your goals.*

- Close your eyes and begin to breathe very slowly and deeply in through your nose and out through your mouth. At the top of your breath hold for three seconds, and then count to five on every out-breath. As you breathe out imagine you are breathing away any nervous tension left in your body.

- Allow your mind to become clear and continue to relax. Let every muscle in your body become loose and relaxed. Take time to allow yourself to drift into a deeply relaxed and centred space. If deep relaxation is new to you, the CD will help you become familiar with going into deeply relaxed states.

■ Once you are in that relaxed space, imagine you now have the ideal job or career that you want, along with all the financial security that it brings. Imagine your new lifestyle clearly. Make your visualisation as detailed and colourful as you can. See yourself clearly in your ideal work situation and imagine it is a reality now. Allow yourself to feel very secure and see yourself coping with any stress with a new inner strength and calm.

■ Focus on this for as long as you wish. Any time you get a negative thought, just allow it to drift away and re-focus on the positive. Then, when you are ready to wake up from the trance, slowly count from one to five and tell yourself you are becoming more awake with each number. When you reach the number five, your eyes will open and you will be back to full waking consciousness with a feeling of total well-being.

■ When you run this visualisation repeatedly for a few weeks, your unconscious mind will soon have a new positive programme that it will respond to automatically. The key is to practise these visualisations often so that you compound them. The more your unconscious mind absorbs these positive pictures and feelings, the quicker the changes will occur.

Summary

✓ **Coping with financial stress** – *looking at the ways financial stress problems cause stress.*

✓ **7 mini steps to get out of debt, release stress about money and become more prosperous** – *a mini programme to help you become debt-free and more abundant.*

✓ **Coping with work stress** – *tips and techniques to help you cope with challenges and stresses in the workplace, deal with difficult people and create a more positive working environment.*

✓ **Creating a prosperous lifestyle** – *a technique to help you to crystallise your work or career ambitions.*

✓ **Being clear about your future.**

✓ **Prosperity visualisation technique.**

STEP 3

De-stress your
home environment

Clearing clutter from your home

To help compound your positive and progressive approach to your finances and relationships, you will also need to create a positive home environment. The 7 steps are a holistic approach and every area will impact the next, so your living space needs to be congruent with your positive attitude to your finances and relationships. A house that is cluttered with possessions or junk can be a cause of stress and may create energy blocks. It is important to create a home environment that is calming and free of clutter. Even if you have kids or limited space, there are many things you can do to de-stress your home.

To minimise stress in your home, you need to create a positive environment that feels fresh and alive. Estate agents use techniques to create a warm, positive feeling in a house to make it more appealing to potential buyers. People often decide to buy houses because of the feeling it creates in them. When you walk into a house that is clutter-free and clean, it makes you feel good. Conversely, have you ever been in a house where the energy feels really dense and cold because nothing has ever been moved? You can actually feel the energy in rooms on an unconscious level. So it is important for your mental and emotional well-being that your home affects you in a positive way.

7 mini steps to de-clutter your home

Step 1. Clearing out clutter and junk is a good starting point for creating a positive home environment. In this day and age we accumulate lots of possessions, many of which we don't really need. Have a good look around your home and start on one room at a time. Books, CDs and DVDs are examples of items we tend to hang on to that create clutter. If you have any books, CDs or DVDs that you have no further use for, or you keep them just for show, then give them away – someone else may benefit from them. Make a checklist of all the items that you could throw away or pass on to someone less fortunate than yourself. Maybe you can sell some of the more valuable possessions that you don't really need anymore? Set aside one day every few months to do this so that you keep your home clear of clutter. Maybe schedule a regular date to do this? This helps the energy of your house to stay fresh.

Step 2. Always avoid getting too attached to personal possessions as this can be unhealthy. Instead, focus on creating an 'easy come, easy go' attitude towards them. As much as we may enjoy our material possessions, we can't take them with us when we shed this mortal coil. Think of them as things you enjoy for now but accept that one day you will let them go. Don't feel that you own things; rather that they are temporarily yours to use now. We all come into this world naked and owning nothing and we shall depart it in the same way. It is important to free yourself from over-attachment to possessions. Get into a regular habit of giving away or selling possessions that you rarely use and that clutter your home.

> 'Desire makes everything blossom; possession makes everything wither and fade.'
>
> **Marcel Proust**

Step 3. Take any clothes you haven't worn in the last six months to the local charity shop. Make this six-month time span a golden rule. The only exception is clothes you keep for very special occasions. When you de-clutter your wardrobe, you create the space for new clothes. Having an evolving wardrobe and changing your clothes often will create a feeling of well-being.

Step 4. Make sure your house is clean. Check your walls, windows and doors are free of spider's webs, stains or dirt. If any rooms are in need of redecorating, give them a lick of paint. This will make a big difference to the way you feel about the room. When rooms are decorated they feel fresh and clean. Start one room at a time and completely spring-clean each room, moving furniture and pictures and other objects as you go. Moving objects around in a room gets rid of energy blocks.

Step 5. Your rooms should be sparsely furnished so that they appear larger and lighter. You can always store stuff you can't bear to part with in your garage or loft, but try to be ruthless in getting rid of objects that take up too much space and serve little purpose. Remember the golden rule: never have overemotional attachments to inanimate objects.

Step 6. Do not allow furniture to block windows, doorways, or access to rooms. Make sure you store things in cupboards and cabinets. For example, your bathroom and kitchen should look sparse, with items you use daily kept in cabinets or cupboards so that shelves and sinks are free of clutter. Add some stylish lamps to your rooms to create a warm lighting effect and remove excessive photos and pictures.

Step 7. Once you have created a feeling of space, adding the odd small plant will help your home to feel more alive. However, don't add too many as this will be counter-productive. Outside your home, if you have a garden, make sure your lawn is neat and regularly cut and your borders edged. Throw away any junk or clutter in the garden and add a plant or two to the front of your house. A new 'Welcome' mat at your front door will add a little warmth.

Space-clearing outline

Space-clearing is not for everyone as it deals with more subtle energies, but I believe it can be another little step towards creating a positive, stress-free atmosphere in your home. More importantly, it can remove any negative energy lurking around. We have all heard the stories of people moving to a new house and having nothing but bad luck while they live there. I once lived in a street like that. It was only a small street, but a number of the residents had serious health problems, some of them fatal. There were also occasional violent disputes between neighbours and various other problems that were out of place in a seemingly nice area. Soon after we moved in, we called in a guy to space-clear our property and I believe it was one of the reasons why we never suffered with the problems that our neighbours did. It felt as though we were cocooned in a positive environment while the mayhem and stress continued outside.

Some of you with a more scientific bent may not be convinced that energies can leave a negative imprint and cause problems. But almost all of us have been somewhere new and had a feeling of déjà vu. Some believe this is because we have been in the same place in a past life, or because we are responding to the subtle energy from events that occurred in the past. Old battlegrounds, where there were many casualties, can have a tangible sense of despair and gloom; graveyards have their own unique atmosphere. We could say this is just because intellectually we know we should feel sad when we visit such places, but animals also respond to the energy in places like this. Near where I live, there is a new upmarket estate that has been built on the site of an old airfield that was bombed many times during the war. It is a huge estate that has been elegantly designed, but oddly there are almost no birds to be seen there even though there are plenty of parks and woodland.

Space-clearing case study

Some believe that people can leave a vibrational imprint on a house. I became aware of this possibility when my wife and I visited her sister and husband, who owned a remote pub in the Scottish Highlands. Since our relatives had moved into this pub, their previously stable relationship had gone rapidly downhill. They were constantly fighting and arguing, which was something they hadn't done before moving in. We had gone up for a relaxing break but we got caught in the crossfire and a relaxing holiday soon turned into a stressful one. We also discovered that two couples who had previously owned the pub had gone through the same thing – both had eventually got divorced. Incidentally, the pub was called the Allargue Arms and stands overlooking the site of an ancient battleground!

My wife, who had a little knowledge of space-clearing, suggested to her sister that she could try to space-clear the pub. My sister-in-law thought it wouldn't hurt to give it a go as long as we didn't tell her husband. He is a doctor from a strictly scientific background and had he found out, would have become convinced my wife was a witch and wanted her dunked in the local pond!

Anyway, my wife did her clearing thing and I kid you not, from that day on, the arguments stopped and my sister-in-law and her husband were back to their old selves. My sister-in-law was amazed, as we all were. Whatever it was my wife did, she shifted some of the old blocked energy in that place and the tenants responded positively to their new cleansed environment. Instances like this have to be more than a coincidence. My brother-in-law knew nothing about the space-clearing but still responded to the changes positively, which cancels out the placebo possibility.

If you are not convinced that space-clearing is a viable step in creating a positive environment, why not give it a go anyway? Adopt the 'don't knock it until you've tried it' attitude. It certainly won't do any harm. You can either call in a space-clearing specialist or you can learn more about space clearing your home from books by experts in this area, such as Karen Kingston. See page 181 for more information.

Feng Shui outline

Once again, Feng Shui is not something for everyone, but I can't think that a technique like this would have survived over thousands of years if there wasn't something in it. It comes from the ancient Chinese art of placement with the aim of achieving harmony, comfort and balance in the environment, which then flows through and into your life. The literal translation of Feng Shui is wind-water and it follows the alignment of the natural currents and elements of the earth and can create harmony in your environment by using the specific placement of objects to create a positive energy or a healthy flow of chi. Think of it as like a spiritual interior design that can enhance your home or office and impact upon your physical and spiritual well-being.

In Feng Shui, each area of the house represents specific areas in your life, such as abundance, relationships, fame and reputation, etc. If, for example, the relationships area in your house is full of clutter and broken items, this may also reflect in your actual personal relationships. The clutter and broken items will be symbolic of what is going on in your relationships. If you have re-occurring problems with certain aspects of your life, you may want to look at how they relate to the areas in your house as dictated by Feng Shui principles. I don't have enough knowledge in this area to suggest a Feng Shui treatment plan, but I can relay a personal case study of how Feng Shui made an impact on me.

Feng Shui case study

I come from quite a down-to-earth south London background and so I don't tend to just believe in these things without question. But, when you look for guidance or proof of the validity of such things, it often comes to you in subtle ways. I was once given proof of the power of Feng Shui in a less than subtle way. In the late 1990s, I began producing my first hypnotherapy tapes and CDs, which went on to sell hundreds of thousands and become best-sellers. I had started producing them in a tiny back bedroom on a basic recording set-up, then sold them to local stores. It wasn't long before they started to take off and I soon had a full-time business on my hands.

With the business growing, I was able to buy a bigger

house. A few months after moving into our new home, I sourced a new cassette-duplicating company. I placed a trial order for 1,000 duplicated copies of a cassette title of mine called *Deep Sleep*. I later discovered that when they duplicate at these plants they have one long cassette tape on a large drum, which gets spliced and loaded into the small cassette cases. When a run has finished, they cut the tape and the next order goes through. After they ran my *Deep Sleep* title, the next audio on the drum was by a Northern comedian called Roy Chubby Brown. For those of you unfamiliar with him, he is probably the bluest comedian in the UK. He makes Billy Connolly sound like a vicar.

Unfortunately, the quality control at the duplicating plant wasn't up to scratch that day and Chubby Brown's recording also got transferred to fifty or so of my cassettes. When I took delivery of the 1,000 cassettes, the packaging all looked fine. There were no visual clues that there was a problem and I unwittingly sent my *Deep Sleep* tapes out into the nation's bookstores with fifty of them imbued with the bluest language you can imagine. If your grandmother heard the first ten seconds, it would finish her off, and it wasn't long before bookstores began calling with horror stories from their customers. They wanted to know why I was using abusive language on my relaxation recordings. One store called to say that an elderly man came into the store in tears because of the stress caused by my tape. He had lain down at bedtime with his headphones on, expecting to be guided to sleep, only to be verbally abused.

I was horrified and made monumental efforts to recall all of the sleep tapes before my career completely disappeared down the plughole. One major chain told me that if any more of these recordings showed up on their shelves they would boycott my products. I was gutted, as the whole thing was out of my control. It was at this moment that my wife made an interesting Feng Shui discovery – in the studio of our new house, my fame and reputation area was full of old junk and desperately needed clearing. The layout of the room also meant the energy was going out of the window – much like my reputation! My wife suggested that clearing it might solve the problem and I agreed that it wouldn't hurt to try. After we did this, almost to the day, no more of the problem tapes showed up and my business survived. My fame and reputation was prevented from going 'out of the window' and from that moment on I became a believer in Feng Shui! (I still can't look at Roy Chubby Brown without bearing my teeth though!)

I can laugh at the memory now as there was no lasting damage. The elderly gent recovered and we sent him a load of free tapes and he became convinced we were good guys after all. Now, whenever I move into a new home or work space, or even buy a new car, I always space-clear it first then do the Feng Shui thing.

After space-clearing your environment, you may want to call in a Feng Shui expert to completely de-stress your home because it is quite an involved practise. There are some references on page 181 if you want to learn more about Feng Shui.

Developing your creativity

It has been said that television has become the drug of the modern age: 'the opiate of the modern masses'. Almost every household has at least one television and kids are reared watching television from a young age. It is an easy source of entertainment. With hundreds of channels available night and day, there is always something available that will pique your interest. However, watching television is a passive activity that does not stimulate your brain in the same way as, say, when you read a book. Everything is presented to you via a screen and this passive form of entertainment requires you to use little imagination. However, when you read a book, your imagination creates its own pictures and you stimulate the creative part of your mind. The same happens when you paint, draw, play an instrument or write poetry or songs. When you engage in these types of activities you are using the right hemisphere of your brain. This is where your

> 'Your vision will become clear only when you can look into your own heart. Who looks outside, dreams, who looks inside awakes.'
> **Carl Gustav Jung**

creativity lies, and your creativity is infinite. No one has a limited amount of creativity; it is a case of the more you use it, the more creative you become. Songwriters and poets often say that the more they write, the better their work becomes. The more you regularly engage in creative pursuits, the more you stimulate your creativity.

There are two hemispheres of the brain. In simple terms, the left hemisphere is responsible for logical, analytical thinking and the right hemisphere is responsible for imagination and creative thinking. In today's world, we tend to use our analytical, logical left brain much more often than our creative right brain. But it is the right brain that holds the key to connecting with your inner talents and creativity. When you are regularly expressing your creativity, you will feel happier and less stressed, and so it is important to cultivate use of your creative brain functions. You can do this when you use self-hypnosis and visualisation. Einstein said, 'Imagination is more important than knowledge. Knowledge is limited. Imagination encircles the world.' He attributed many of his greatest theories to right-brain activity and said being in trance states helped him to formulate his great ideas.

Getting a balance between watching television and being creative is important in this day and age. Television shows a lot of negative images, especially when harrowing documentaries and news stories are broadcast. As we have seen before, this can create fear and insecurity in people's minds, which can cause stress. So remember to be selective about the programmes you watch. Most of the time I avoid the news and only record programmes that are inspiring or educational or make me laugh. . . . Alright, and I watch the football!

De-stress tip – become more creative and therefore less stressed

■   Inject more creativity into your life. Why not learn to play a musical instrument or take up painting, creative writing or some other creative pursuit?

Creative right-brain pursuits are such a great way to de-stress and relax. If you have children, try to limit their TV viewing and get them into the habit of reading more or doing something else that is creative. If you get this right from an early age, it can have a profound knock-on effect as your children will undoubtedly grow up to become brighter, more creative adults. If you create a healthy habit early on, it becomes the norm and children don't question it – that is, until they go to school and mix with other kids!

Visualising a positive and happy home

The following script will help you to feel more positive and creative in your home environment.

> *I suggest you read the following script through a few times so that you learn it well before you practise it. Feel free to adapt it to suit your own aims.*

- Go to a quiet room where there are no distractions. Take a moment to get in a comfortable position, close your eyes and focus your attention on your breathing. Then begin breathing slowly and deeply – in through your nose and out through your mouth. Breathe away any tension left in your body with every slow out-breath, and allow yourself to relax more and more.

- Continue this breathing pattern a dozen or more times and just clear away any unwanted thoughts so that your mind becomes still and quiet. Just focus on the stillness of the moment.

■ To guide yourself deeper into a trance, silently count down from ten to one. Keep your breathing slow and deep. Leave about five seconds between each number and feel every muscle in your body relax more and more.

■ In this stillness, imagine you are looking into large crystal ball and in the crystal ball you can see your house. Visualise a very happy, positive environment and see a white protective light all around your house. Imagine this white light permeates every room in your home and that it has special healing energies.

■ As the whole picture becomes larger and clearer, imagine yourself stepping into this magical image as though it is a reality and as though you are looking out through your own eyes. As you do this, you feel that everything in your home is harmonious and in balance. You have become happy and content and you are expressing yourself in many new and creative ways. Your relationship with every-one around you is loving and harmonious and there is so much love in your life. Hold this picture for a while and make it big, bright and clear. Really feel it is a reality for you now. Affirm to yourself that these feelings will stay with you.

■ Now, in this relaxed and receptive state, you can silently recite the following affirmations, which will help you to feel more creative and inspired. State the affirmations in the present tense with real belief and conviction. When you state these phrases, draw the words inside you and really believe they are a reality. Put your feelings into it as you express each affirmation. You can adapt the affirmations or add your own present tense phrases. These are just some examples:

* I have a positive and happy home environment.
* I feel creative and inspired at home and in my work.
* I manifest wonderful things in my life.
* I express my creativity in many different ways.
* I take on new challenges with a positive attitude.

■ When you are ready to finish, allow your mind to clear for a minute, then count slowly upwards from one to ten. Open your eyes when you reach the number eight and at the number ten you will come back to full waking consciousness:
1...2...3...4...5...6...7...8...9...10...

■ Repeat this daily and you will find new, creative ideas will come to you now that you have opened up this channel. It may be that this will manifest in getting new ideas out of the blue a day or two later. Practise this exercise when-ever you need inspiration. Many creative geniuses have produced their greatest works when they were accessing their unconscious minds. Even as a child, Mozart could hear a long, complex piece of music for the first time and then play it note for note in an instant. This type of ability comes from the creative right-brain functions.

Summary

✓ **Clearing clutter from your home** – *why it is important to de-clutter your home.*

✓ **7 mini steps to de-clutter your home** – *follow the 7 mini steps to a de-cluttered home.*

✓ **Space-clearing outline** – *a brief understanding of how space-clearing works.*

✓ **Space-clearing case study** – *an example of why it is important to clear blocked energy and create a fresh, positive feeling in your home.*

✓ **Feng Shui outline** – *a brief understanding of how Feng Shui works.*

✓ **Feng Shui case study.**

✓ **Developing your creativity** – *taking steps to develop your creativity and how to use it in your home life.*

✓ **Visualising a positive and happy home** – *a self-hypnosis technique.*

STEP 4

De-stress your relationships

Family relationships

Relationships can be a common source of stress and creating positive, harmonious relationships is not always easy, especially within families. Fifty years ago families stayed in regular, close contact for life. People generally partnered for life and, even when their children grew up and started their own families, they usually lived nearby, so there was a sense of stability, and families were in regular communication.

It is when communication breaks down that problems often begin. Disagreements and disputes can usually be resolved by sitting down, airing feelings and listening. Not always, but more often than not, a good old heart-to-heart can do the trick. In times gone by, families supported each other more and pulled together in times of crisis. Nowadays people are more independent and have many more choices and options. People don't feel they have to stay stuck in unhappy marriages and may have children with more than one partner. The divorce rate is at an all-time high and it is common for children to be raised by a single parent or with an extra step-parent. Many good, older family traditions have been eroded in our fast-paced modern life. Families don't always spend mealtimes together, which was always a time for communication. There was always a solid logic behind these traditions. Many have been lost and forgotten, and replaced by the need for constant entertainment and stimulation.

General relationships

Relationships can become problematic because people don't always live up to our expectations and we don't always live up to theirs. If you think about someone in your life who you have relationship problems with, the problems will have arisen because you believe they are acting incorrectly, and vice versa. But, if you can adopt a more liberal attitude and accept that people will be a pain in the arse now and again, it can help. I'm not suggesting it will solve all problems, but it can alleviate tensions. If it is possible, sit down with the person you have the problem with and communicate. When you do this, make sure the territory is neutral

> 'My religion is simple, my religion is kindness.'
> **Dalai Llama**

and there is no one else around. Don't have the sit-down at your house or theirs, go to a pub or coffee bar that neither of you frequent, and talk. If this doesn't resolve differences, you can always go to a relationship counsellor who can help you get to the bottom of your unresolved issues. This is a great way of resolving relationship problems as a good counsellor can cut through the crap and point out where the problems lie with no pre-judgement.

Direct communication is the key to resolving disputes. Hoping the other person will change or suddenly see things your way is unlikely unless you communicate. The following mini programme will give you some pointers to help you communicate effectively and hopefully heal the relationship.

5 mini steps to heal relationship conflicts

These steps are generalised and will not fit every situation, so adapt them for your own needs. It will help if you have a strategy before you aim to resolve a conflict.

Step 1. Ask the person with whom you are in conflict if they would like to meet you to discuss the problem. It is preferable to work with one person at a time.

Step 2. If they agree, meet them at a neutral public venue, like a pub or coffee bar. It must be a public place that neither of you frequent and preferably equidistant from your home and theirs. If you live in the same house, go for a walk together in an uplifting place like a woodland or quiet park.

Step 3. Before the meeting, project a feeling of love towards the other person. Use the de-stress technique – 'develop a big-heart and more compassion' on page 87. Even though this love may not be reciprocated, do not worry. Just send them a genuine feeling of unconditional love and try to hold onto that feeling throughout your discussions, even if you still disagree or argue. This maybe challenging, but it will help you to express yourself more positively and you will feel better for it afterwards.

Step 4. When you meet face-to-face, greet them with a genuine compliment. Nothing too gushing, just a 'you're looking well' or something similar will suffice. Start on a positive note and try to be respectful throughout the meeting, even if it gets heated. When you talk, look them in the eye and stay strong and positive.

> 'Honest differences are often a healthy sign of progress.'
> **Mahatma Gandhi**

Step 5. If you have issues to get across, say them along these lines: 'I am really sorry we have got to this point and that we don't agree, but I am here because I genuinely want to get rid of the bad feeling between us. You may not like everything I have to say, but I'm going to be honest and say how I feel, as I really want us to resolve our dispute and build a more positive relationship. Please hear me out before you make a judgement'. Then state your case with honesty and clarity and speak from your heart if you need to. Keep your approach warm and sincere and hold the feeling of love throughout. When the other person speaks, encourage them to speak from their heart and relay *their* truth. Listen carefully to what they say and try and understand *their* needs. This will help you build bridges and hopefully resolve the conflict.

Opening your heart and mind

If all else fails to heal the relationship, you can use the following De-stress tip and the Creating Harmonious Relationships technique at the end of this chapter. The following tip is about feeling more warmth and compassion towards people. Don't think of opening your heart as weak – being more loving and compassionate will make you stronger and wiser over time. This will also help you to improve your self-esteem.

De-stress tip – develop a big heart and more compassion

- Whenever you are out and about, make a habit of projecting a positive feeling of love to everyone you pass by. Imagine a strong feeling of love coming from your heart and reaching their hearts, and silently focus on the word 'love'. When you do this, avoid judgement or discrimination. Practise this technique with anyone and everyone: family, friends, acquaintances and strangers.

There is a great line in a classic song by The Doors: 'People are strange, when you're a stranger'. How often have you met someone and been put off by the way they spoke or looked, but warmed to them when you got to know them a little? When you get into the habit of projecting positive feelings without prejudice to everyone you meet, this will open your heart and you will change the way you feel towards people. You will become naturally more compassionate and loving and, importantly, you will also be attracting more love back into your life. The universal law of attraction states: 'What you give out will come back to you.' This is a great technique for helping you to feel good inside and generally improving your relationships with people.

You still need to be aware that no matter how loving you are, there are some people who will not reflect love back to you. If you come across people like this, you must use the white light protection technique on page 56 to avoid your energy being drained. Everyone is attracted to big-hearted people and, when you become more loving, you also become a magnet for people. As with all things, a small minority of the energy you attract will be of the wrong sort, so be aware of this and establish firm boundaries with people if you need to; don't be afraid to push people away from you if they are an energy drain. When you learn to love people, it should come from a place of strength, not a woolly, drippy thing where you totally subjugate yourself. Be loving, compassionate and big-hearted, but at the same time be strong and never let people crap on you. That is real strength.

> 'If someone does not smile at you, be generous and offer your own smile. Nobody needs a smile more than the one that cannot smile to others.'
>
> **Dalai Llama**

De-stress your relationships
with your children

In the UK, family life has become very fragmented and communication breakdowns are at the heart of many relationship problems. Today there are serious problems with juvenile delinquency. Every town and city in the UK has displaced teenagers hanging around on street corners looking for trouble. I know because I was once one of them! This doesn't happen so much in countries like Spain and Italy where the family unit still holds great importance. In these countries, the matriarchal figures are strong and command respect. Fathers are often present and communicative with their children. I am generalising a bit here, but the bottom line is that when parents are involved with their children and give them time, the children grow up well balanced and better able to cope with life's challenges.

> 'Children need models rather than critics.'
> **Joseph Joubert**

If you can communicate with your children at each step of their development, you will be able to influence their behaviour. It doesn't mean you will always like what they are doing, but if the communication channels are open then you always have a hope of getting through to them. Talking to and understanding your children is very important, and you should never give up on them. I was expelled from school at fifteen and told I was the worst kid they'd had in the school for ten years. They said I would amount to nothing. Now look, I am writing books and helping people!

De-stress tip – cultivate the communication habit

- Avoid watching TV at mealtimes. If it is possible, make a habit of having at least one meal a day with your family or whoever you live with. Use that time to really communicate and to resolve problems if you need to. Remember, positive communication is the key to having good relationships.

Children respond to their environment, especially at home. I never met a bad kid who didn't have inadequate parents. Poor parents often simply lack the understanding of their children's changing needs. In my hypnotherapy practice, I have had parents bring their children to me because they need help with bad behaviour, but the parents are invariably a big part of the problem. When parents give their children love, security and understanding, the children prosper and flourish. I know it is not always easy to achieve this, especially when parents divorce or separate, but you should always put your children first: before your ego, your needs and your wants. Even if your partner doesn't do the same, you should lead by example.

One of the fathers of modern psychology, Sigmund Freud, had some strange theories, but also some very valid ones. One of his better notions was that children go through a number of specific stages of development in their journey from infancy to adolescence to adulthood. If any of those stages are dysfunctional or problematic, a part of the child becomes psychologically stuck at that stage of their development. The next time you see an adult acting like a child, you can bet your bottom dollar it is the child part of them acting up.

Adults who often display childish traits more often than not have had problems with their development at one or more stages during childhood. They may not even realise it is this part of them that creates their dysfunctional or destructive patterns of behaviour, but there is always a starting point for our idiosyncrasies and personality traits. We are very subtle beings and our childhood conditioning creates behaviour blueprints that remain with us for the rest of our lives.

It is possible to overcome destructive patterns in adult life through various therapies. In my hypnotherapy work, I always find that regressing people to the root cause of the problem is a powerful way to release and overcome destructive patterns of behaviour or fears and anxieties. Imagine, though, how great it would be if we could avoid passing problems on to our children. Imagine, for a moment, if the next generation of parents were all equally enlightened: strong and disciplined, but also compassionate and sensitive; nurturing, caring, loving and always putting their children's needs first. Imagine if this generation of parents also gave their children huge self-belief and confidence and taught them to be respectful, positive, independent and to live life to the full. If we could collectively achieve this in a single generation, we would wipe out delinquency, crime, conflict and even war. A little idealistic, I know, but why not strive to do your bit and take your parenting skills up to another level. It is the most underrated job in the world. When you genuinely do a good job as a parent, the rewards are huge. In the fullness of your lifetime, your parenting efforts will far outweigh the rewards of a good career or making money.

7 mini steps to improve your parenting skills

If you don't have children yourself, you can either skip this section or you may want to pass on some of these tips to someone you know who has children.

Step 1. The one thing that children want from you is guidance and boundaries. They may not know it or realise it, but they will feel more secure when they have rules and boundaries to adhere to. Children are learning from day one and you, as their parent, are their teacher. By giving them clear boundaries as to what is right or wrong, you are teaching them acceptable behaviour and respect. They will feel much more secure when you show strength and guidance.

Step 2. Whenever you set a boundary, always tell your children the reason behind it. When you explain your reasoning, speak to them with respect and compassion, but at the same time be strong and firm. If you want to get your child into a positive behaviour pattern, tell them positive stories about yourself when you were their age. Children love stories, and a bit of creative licence here is fine if it's a means to a good end. They will relate to your stories and it will help them to understand you and where you came from. They will connect with you and understand why you are asking them to behave in a certain way. Be creative with your kids and teach them well. You will have stories to teach them at any age, as you will have been there yourself.

■

Step 3. From day one, always encourage your children and let them believe they can achieve anything. Young children still believe in magic and have unlimited imaginations. As adults we can learn a lot from them. If you are constantly encouraging your kids and empowering them from an early age, they will prosper and flourish throughout their lives. One of the best things you can give your children is a strong feeling of self-belief. You do this by encouraging them and nurturing them through every stage of their development. You can never do too much of this with children, as they thrive on encouragement. Tell them often that they are good, clever, smart, funny, bright and talented, and that is what they will become. You need to pick your moments and impart your praise in the right context, but that is the gist of it. Do not underestimate the power of your words.

■

Step 4. Needless to say, you should *never* criticise your children or use destructive language when speaking to them. Kids are like sponges and they absorb everything. If you make a habit of telling your kids they are useless, stupid or hopeless, it will become self-fulfilling. Simply cut out any such language from your vocabulary when you speak to your children. Make that a golden rule. And never shout at them because of the mood *you* are in. If they play up, always count to ten. Then tell them in a firm and controlled way how you want them to behave. Make sure you and your partner never argue or discuss your child's behaviour in front of them. Discuss your differences in private and always present a united front. This will stop your children playing you off against each other or taking sides. Animal groups have pecking orders and it should be the same in your household. As the parents, you should always be running the show and your kids must respect you.

Step 5. Have fun with your kids. Children thrive on fun and adventure at all ages. If you get into the habit of playing with your kids from a young age, you will build a strong bond with them that will last for life. There are times to be their mum or dad, but there are also times when you can be their mate and have fun with them. Make this a habit through every stage of their development. There is nothing more liberating than being silly and having playful fun with your kids. It will also connect you to a carefree, fun part of yourself. So make it a habit and enjoy being with your kids.

Step 6. Children go through many growth stages, both physically and emotionally. At some stages in their development, your children may well begin to distance themselves from you. This can manifest in them suddenly becoming obnoxious or rebellious and argumentative. This is common in teenagers. When this occurs, don't judge them or jump all over them. Give them a bit of space and try to understand what is at the bottom of any sudden changes in their behaviour. Being a bolshie teenager and rebelling against your parents is completely normal. They are naturally breaking away from you and trying to form their own identity. It is healthy and should be encouraged, even if it gets you down. They will always come back to you if the bonds are strong. So handle them carefully at all times and cut them a bit of slack when they need it. None of us are perfect and your children will be no different.

> 'Children begin by loving their parents; as they grow older they judge them; sometimes they forgive them.'
> **Oscar Wilde**

Step 7. Most importantly, let your kids know you love them. You may think they already know that you love them, but they will believe and accept it more readily when you actually say it to them. Children thrive on love and security and you can't give them enough of both. Dads generally have more difficulty in this area than mums, but if you get into the habit of saying to your kids 'I love you', it soon becomes the norm and not an embarrassment. Obviously, choose your moments, but do get this message across in a clear way regularly. It will also help your kids to know that you are proud of them. It means a lot to them; that is why they are always showing you stuff and telling you what they have done. I still do it with my parents and I'm forty-four! So pick your moments and tell them and watch them soar. Nurturing and empowering your kids is the most important thing you will do in your life, without question.

In summary

Hopefully there are a few pointers here to help you. As a parent myself, I know it is not always plain sailing, but you must never give up on your kids. Even if they display brattish or unacceptable behaviour, try to understand them and keep the communication lines open. Communicating with your children at all times is so important. Even when their behaviour is bad, keep talking to them and listening to them. There are some great books on this subject that will give you a greater understanding of the way children develop and, as a result, help you to become a better parent (see page 181).

Divorce case study

When I split from my first wife, we were in our mid-twenties and my son was a baby. However, we both agreed to put our disputes aside and to put our son first. My wife moved back to her mum's and we lived fifty miles apart, but I made the 100-mile round trip at least once a week without fail for well over ten years. Even though I was broke and my cars weren't always up to the trip, I never missed a week. I was always welcomed by my ex and her family and had great communication with my son through every step of his childhood. I also made the most of the one day a week I had with him, as it was precious time. Although my son grew up in a single parent household, he is now, at nineteen, a very well-balanced, positive boy with a million and one plans for his future. I am still good friends with my ex-wife and I continue to support her as she has been a wonderful mother to my son. She even comes on holidays with my son, my wife and myself. It is a bit weird going away with two wives, but they are great friends and people often say how nice this is. Although we divorced, we put our egos aside and worked hard to give my son an example of how to have a good relationship in spite of our differences.

I often see people destroying their children with their own selfish needs and wants. It makes me cringe. They always blame the other partner and claim they want the best for their kids. As a teenager, I once ended up in a prison cell because of my parents' fighting, but that story is for another book. It wasn't nice, though, and I got well and truly caught in their crossfire. If your partner is difficult, you don't have to lower yourself to the same level of behaviour. If you are in a situation where you are not on speaking terms with your ex, use the Creating Harmonious Relationships technique below, with them in mind. Even if this feels difficult to do, give it a go for the sake of your children. It is always the kids that suffer when parents fight and quarrel. If you cut out the lip service and *genuinely* act with your children's best interests at heart, you will always win their respect in the end. Children can be manipulated but in the fullness of time, they will usually see the truth and know who was acting in their best interests and who was not.

You can apply this rule to a break-up, even if you don't have kids. Sometimes the path of least resistance is the best one. It takes two people to have a fight and turning the other cheek is often the best response. I am not suggesting you become submissive, but if there is conflict and dispute, try to rise above it. Act with honesty and integrity, even if the other person does not. There is a real strength in acting that way when faced with hostility. In the end, you will feel better for not lowering yourself to the level of others. In subsequent relationships you will attract partners who are like you, thereby so cultivating good ethics and a big-hearted attitude.

Creating Harmonious Relationships technique

Read the following script through a few time before you practise it. This is a wonderful technique to help you improve relationships with one or more people. It will also help you to feel more love and compassion. As always, practise it regularly to get the best results.

- Once again, take yourself off to a quiet room where there are no distractions. Close your eyes and focus your attention on your breathing. Begin breathing slowly and deeply until you feel relaxed and centred.

- Become aware of your heart and imagine it is filled with pure white light. A white light that resonates with unconditional love, the kind of love a mother feels for her baby. Feel this white light of love growing in your heart. Imagine the white light expanding out from your heart so that it begins to fill your whole body. Feel a strong sense of love and compassion for all things.

▦ Imagine the white light expanding, filling your entire body and spreading out into your aura and further still. As though this spark of light has grown so strong that it now projects out and away from you in every direction. Make this deep feeling of love and compassion in your heart grow stronger and stronger, and imagine that the white light grows ever brighter as it reaches further and further.

▦ Visualise your white light of unconditional love reaching out now and engulfing others. It can be to people you know or to individuals who you want to improve relations with. Or it can be general. Imagine the white light stemming from your heart embracing others, and feel a strong sense of love for these people. Feel a deep compassion for their struggles and troubles, seeing their faults and weaknesses as manifestations of difficulties in their lives. Connect with a powerful feeling of love and compassion while you are in this deeply relaxed state.

▦ At this point, you can state the following affirmations to compound this feeling of love and compassion. State the affirmations as a reality now in the present tense. These are some examples, but please adapt and add your own to suit your needs:

  ✳ I love to develop positive relationships with people.
  ✳ I am compassionate and understanding.
  ✳ I give and receive love easily.

▦ When you state your affirmations, draw the words inside you and really believe they are a reality. Put real positive feeling into each phrase and totally believe in what you are affirming. The more you believe in the phrases, the stronger they will become. As always, you will need to practise the technique a few times and repeat the affirmations regularly to get the best results.

- When you are ready to finish, allow your mind to clear and count slowly upwards from one to ten, and open your eyes and come back to full waking consciousness: 1...2...3...4...5...6...7...8...9...10... Wide awake and loved-up!

Summary

✓ **Family relationships** – *looking at family relationships in the modern age.*

✓ **General relationships** – *looking at relationships in general in the modern age.*

✓ **5 mini steps to heal relationship conflicts** – *strategies to help you resolve conflicts in any relationship.*

✓ **Opening your heart and mind** – *a technique to help you develop more love and compassion.*

✓ **De-stress your relationships with your children** – *understanding your kids and building bonds with them.*

7 mini steps to improve your parenting skills – *techniques to help you improve your relationships with your children at every stage of their development.*

Divorce case study.

Creating harmonious relationships technique.

STEP 5

De-stress your health

Stress-free health

Health worries can be a source of stress for many people, especially as we get older. However, worrying about health is completely counter-productive and will only increase stress. Instead, you need to take positive action to become healthier and fitter, whatever age you are. You can do this quite easily and without struggle, as becoming fit and healthy is something you can learn to enjoy doing. On reaching

> 'The art of medicine consists in amusing the patient while nature cures the disease.'
> **Voltaire**

middle age, I decided I was not going to possess middle-aged man breasts and a spare tyre like so many of my male friends and acquaintances. I instead made a conscious decision to become fit and healthy. Rather than joining a gym and going hard at it, only to get bored and quit after a month or so, initially I created a holistic approach to my health and reached levels of fitness that I thought were only achievable in my younger years.

I now have the same 28-inch waist size as I did in my teens

and I rarely get colds, bugs, headaches or any other common ailments that afflict so many. Now, I know you are probably thinking what a smug so-and-so, but I tell you this not to gloat, but so that I can show you, through the examples that follow, how to create the same level of stress-free health. That is, to be fit and healthy, look younger and avoid getting sick or ill. I believe that if you have a strong immune system, you can go through your whole life without suffering any illness or disease. Your body has better defence mechanisms for fighting disease than any drug ever created. Personally, I don't believe in medicinal drugs and I haven't taken any for years. Most drugs simply suppress symptoms and do not cure disease. When your body is healthy, it can easily fight off disease without any outside help. This chapter will include a number of techniques to help you create optimum health. Don't worry if you don't want to follow every guideline, but do try to stick to the 80/20 rule: if 80 per cent of the time you are doing the good stuff, that is eating well and exercising, then you can allow 20 per cent of the time for the odd guilt-free overindulgence.

Detoxing your body

If you are worried about the state of your health, you need to take action now. One of the fastest ways to improve your health, lose a few pounds and have more energy is to detox. Detoxing your system will flush out toxins from your body that have built up because of poor diet and other effects. When you become toxic, you are very prone to disease because

illness flourishes in a toxic body.
Your body can become toxic for
a number of reasons. The most
common are overexposure to
radiation from mobile phones,
computers, and so on, and con-
sumption of food and drinks
that are loaded with chemicals

> 'Nothing will benefit
> human health and
> increase the chances for
> survival of life on Earth as
> much as the evolution to
> a vegetarian diet.'
> **Albert Einstein**

and additives. This is the major cause of high toxic levels in
the body, since most food nowadays is full of chemicals and
additives. (This is because food becomes more profitable if it
has a long shelf life and the way food manufacturers achieve
this is by preserving it with chemicals, salt or sugar.)

One in three people now get cancer, and one in three
people have diabetes. Right now, I can think of dozens of
people I know with these diseases. Cancer and diabetes are
reaching epidemic levels and it is largely because most people
regularly eat food loaded with chemicals and sugar. The food
industry is a billion-dollar industry and most food producers
are being forced by supermarkets to produce food as cheaply
as possible. In our commercial world, all big businesses have
one simple aim: to maximise profits by buying or producing
as cheaply as possible. It is the way of the world and the food
industry is no different. But if you are eating food day in, day
out, which is packed with chemicals that your body doesn't
recognise, you are going to become very toxic and vulnerable
to disease.

Sorry if I have scared you, but knowledge is power, and
with a little knowledge, you can make more informed decisions about the food and drinks you consume. If you want to
de-stress your health, eating good food is an absolute must.

There can be a lot to learn in this area, as there are many bad guys in the food industry pretending to be good guys. So much unhealthy, low nutritional food is sold to the masses as healthy food. It can be a bit of a minefield getting to the truth of it all. A good rule of thumb is that if it has been processed or comes out of a tin, don't eat it. On page 181 I have recommended a few good books that will help you to become more knowledgeable on this subject.

Creating a new, healthy eating lifestyle is not always straightforward, but the easiest way to start is to detox. That means spending a week or two living on nothing but fresh water, pure juices and salads. Before you recoil in horror, suspend your decision for a moment. It is a challenge, for sure, but one where the rewards can be life changing. I have spent weeks detoxing and it is fantastic. I wish I had known about it years ago. You may feel a bit rough during the first two or three days, but this is because your body is letting go of toxins and poisons lurking around in your system. After a few more days, you will start to feel more energised and alert. Personally, I always feel brighter and more alive after a detox. Having a little discipline in your life now and again is very good for your soul.

On page 181 I recommend a great detox book by the fitness guru Jason Vale that will work wonders for your health. A simple week-long detox plan can also help you eliminate addictions to nicotine, caffeine, alcohol, sugar, etc. Once you break the habit and clear your system of toxins, you will have no desire to go back to the old destructive addiction. It will also help you to lose weight, increase your energy and, at the end of the week, your eyes will sparkle like a film star's. So come on, what are you waiting for?

There are other ways to avoid toxins. If you can, add a good water filter to your tap water supply. I have a five-stage reverse osmosis water filter that filters every chemical out of our tap water. It even takes the good minerals out, but these are minimal and you will get these minerals elsewhere if your diet is good. It costs about £200, but it will give you very pure, healthy tap water. Some of the cheaper filters won't work as well, but anything is better than nothing. Tap water today is rather unhealthy and full of chemicals and other nasty additives that are not good for your brain and body, so drinking filtered or bottled water is a must. If you drink bottled water, make sure it is from a glass bottle and not from a plastic bottle, as the plastic can react with the water. It is easy to become fanatical, so apply the 80/20 rule. When you have the knowledge, you can decide for yourself. Personally, I even use a water filter on my home shower as we even take in chemicals through our skin when showering. The shower filter is more basic, but it extracts most of the chlorine and it is another little step I take to avoid toxins.

We live in a very toxic world. Our air and water supplies are often polluted, and the manufactured food and drinks we consume are loaded with toxin-producing chemicals. We are also surrounded by electromagnetic radiation in our homes and workspaces. You don't need to be a rocket scientist to figure out why cancer is such an omnipresent disease. So, logically, if you can minimise your exposure to toxins then you are going to be healthier and less prone to sickness. Take conscious steps now to de-stress your health by avoiding as many of the things that make you toxic as possible.

Healthy eating tips

Once you have finished your detox week, you will not want to go back to any bad habits and you will feel completely different about food. You will feel so good that your desire to eat only healthy food will be very strong. Detoxing is a great way to change the way you feel about food or to begin a new

> 'Thou should eat to live; not live to eat.'
> **Socrates**

healthy eating lifestyle. Try eating a chocolate gateau after a week-long detox and it will make you want to gag!

If you want to lose a few pounds, never use the word 'diet' again to describe a new healthy eating plan. The word 'diet' is laced with emotion and is associated with struggle and hardship. You don't need to go on a diet to lose a few pounds and become healthy; you simply need to create a mindset where you feel good about eating small amounts of healthy food. If your mind believes this is something you enjoy, then eating healthy food is something you will do automatically. Needless to say, you can also programme your mind to dislike sickly sweet, fattening foods. I have produced a hypnotherapy CD that will do this very job for you (there are more details on page 182).

The following technique will help you to eradicate sweets, cakes, chocolate, sugar, coffee or any type of junk food from your diet. Focus on one food at a time and use the technique repeatedly over a few days if you need to compound it.

De-stress Technique – hypnotise yourself to dislike fattening junk food permanently

- Think of an unhealthy or fattening food or drink that you would like to avoid permanently. Close your eyes and take a few slow, deep breaths and allow your mind to clear. Take a moment to go inside yourself and totally relax. Then, when you are ready, imagine a plate full of the most putrid, rotting fish. Make this picture clear in your mind's eye and connect with the revolting smell of the fish. Hold back from gagging but make this image and smell very real. Take a moment to do this.

- When you have a clear picture and experience the foul smell in your mind, bring in the fattening food you want to erase from your diet and mix it up with the rotting fish. If, for example, it is chocolate, imagine the chocolate all over the fish, making an even more disgusting smell. If it is coca-cola, imagine one of the fish inside a glass of coke.

- Be creative with this part of the technique, the more vivid you can make this image the more powerful it will be. Allow a good few minutes to absorb this disgusting image and odour into your consciousness, and then allow your mind to become blank. Take a few slow breaths and slowly count to three and open your eyes.

- The next time you think about the food you mixed up with the rotting fish you will feel completely different. You will have lost any desire for that food or drink, and you may even find it quite repulsive now.

You can use this technique to systematically eradicate all bad food habits from your diet. When you eat nutrient-rich, good-quality food, you are feeding your body with the right vitamins, nutrients and minerals. By doing this, you will eat less, as you are giving your body what it needs. Conversely, when you eat food that has been processed or preserved for longevity, the nutritional content of the food will be minimal and your body will struggle to digest the lifeless, chemically enhanced food. Cheap Chinese takeaway food fills you up, but then often leaves you hungry again; this is because most of this type of takeaway food is of low quality and full of monosodium glutamate. The body struggles to digest this type of junk food and then bloats up, which then creates a hunger for real, nutritious, vitamin-rich food.

A high junk food intake can create false hunger and imbalances in the body. Make a habit of shopping for good quality, chemical-free organic food. Organic food is becoming less expensive as the demand rises, and budgeting a little more money to spend on good-quality food should be a number one priority. There are more and more online organic food shops that also offer home delivery services. I have an organic food delivery every week – I find this so much easier than traipsing round supermarkets looking at minute ingredient labels. Incidentally, the reason food ingredient labels are so small is because often the food manufacturers don't want you to know what is in the food – if you knew, you probably wouldn't buy it.

One final thing I would like to add is that having some knowledge about which foods are good for your particular body type and which foods you should avoid is important. I made this discovery recently as I couldn't understand why some days my energy levels were all over the place and I felt foggy-headed. It didn't make sense, since I eat healthy, organic food and exercise regularly, but some days I would feel like I was hung over. After a visit to a nutritionist, I discovered that gluten was making my blood sugar levels rise and sapping my energy. I thought organic cereal in the morning was okay, but for me it had the same affect as drinking two pints of beer. I now avoid gluten in foods and am fine.

De-stress tip – nutrition for your body type

- Make time to seek out a well-qualified nutritionist who will put you on the right road for eating the foods that suit your body type. Even if you have a good diet, a nutritionist can help you to raise your energy levels and become generally healthier by pinpointing the foods you must avoid and the foods that are good for your specific body type.

A holistic approach to exercise and becoming fit

Regular physical activity has many benefits, not least that it is one of the best ways to overcome stress and anxiety. The 'feel good' hormones in your brain, endorphins, which are released when you exercise, help to clear away negative emotions and have a positive effect on your mood. Exercise also increases blood flow to the brain, stimulates the nervous system and triggers the release of adrenalin in the body, which has an uplifting effect. The after-effects of exercise can also help to lower blood pressure, diminish anxiety levels and calm the mind. A good workout will almost always create a feel-good effect, releasing physical stress and tension held in the body by loosening the muscles. By getting your circulation going, you will also allow your body to release toxins. If you feel angry, a brisk walk or jog will help you to feel more calm and composed and in control of your feelings.

There are two ways to achieve optimum physical fitness: eat healthy food and exercise regularly. There are a million and one excuses people make for being overweight, but they are nearly all myths. If you eat healthily and exercise regularly, you become fit, it is a simple as that. Being big-boned, or having a slow metabolism, are lame excuses for being overweight if you do not have a medical condition that predisposes you to putting on weight. If you sit in front of the television night after night and never exercise, you will have a slow metabolism. But if you exercise often, your metabolism will speed up and you will burn calories more easily. You have the power to influence whether you have a fast or slow metabolism. It is not something you are born with or stuck with.

The first step to achieving physical fitness is to become more active. This can start with simply walking more. It is so easy to drive everywhere these days but if you get the opportunity, walk instead. For example, don't get frustrated if you can't park right outside the restaurant or shop you visit, park a few hundred metres away and walk. Look at the lack of parking spaces as an opportunity to get a little exercise. When you incorporate these ideas into your daily life, they become habits that you get into and enjoy. They also cost you very little time and they become a part of your holistic approach to your fitness. It is very pleasant to have a short walk after leaving a restaurant, and it will help you to burn a few calories. Another tip is to avoid escalators and always use the stairs if you can. There is always another way of viewing things and when you reframe your attitude towards exercise, you will

> To climb steep hills requires a slow pace at first.'
> **Shakespeare**

never again moan because a lift is not working or because you can't find a parking space.

When you decide to improve your fitness levels, approach the decision with the mindset that you are creating a new, holistic, healthy lifestyle. So many people put on a few pounds and initially build a strong resolve to get fit, only to give up after three months and drift back to their old unhealthy ways. It is a fact that gymnasiums oversell their memberships because 80 per cent of people who join gyms stop going after three months; if all members of any given gym turned up at once they would not be able to cope. Think of the tortoise and hare fable, where the slow but steady pace of the tortoise brought success. Use this story as your metaphor for long-term success. Work on your fitness slowly by doing a little each day and building up to a level that feels good for you. If you make physical changes too quickly, your mind will take time to adjust to your new body image. If there is incongruence between your mind's perception of your body image and your actual physical state, this can cause problems. This is why crash dieting always fails. The best way to build lasting fitness is to create a holistic approach.

Embarking on new hobbies and pastimes that will help you cultivate your fitness is important. You need to look at activities you enjoy that will help you to become fitter. If you enjoy the gym then go for it, but make sure that when you join you make a commitment with yourself to use the gym regularly throughout the whole year's membership. Swimming,squash, badminton and tennis are all good aerobic exercises and you may decide to incorporate one or more of these sports into your weekly schedule. Find healthy pursuits that you can do regularly and enjoy. Maybe mix up a number of activities, so that you don't get bored with a routine? Once you decide upon the activities you want to take up and regularly participate in, use the motivation exercise technique on page 117 to programme your mind to love your exercise routines. They will then become permanent habits that you look forward to and genuinely enjoy.

Yoga is a wonderful discipline for toning the body, calming the mind and de-stressing. The best way to learn yoga is in a class, but if you don't want to join a class, there are many tutorial DVDs available, see page 182. The beauty of yoga is that once you learn the basics, you can practise the poses any time or place you choose. You can then fit it into your lifestyle. Even a simple ten-minute daily yoga workout will work wonders on your fitness and stress levels.

De-stress tip – start the day with exercise

■ Set your alarm to wake you ten minutes earlier each day and create a daily ten-minute workout to do before breakfast. This can be a mini trampoline or yoga workout or even both, if you fancy a longer workout.

Exercising first thing in the morning is a great habit to get into. It can also be useful to have a number of exercise aids in and around your house. I have a mini trampoline in my house and a large one in the garden. Just ten minutes a day bouncing up and down provides a great cardio-vascular work out. If you don't have the resources or the space for too many exercise machines, then buy an exercise ball, which is great for sit-ups and many other workouts. I have a number of these things in my house and have created a ten-minute workout that I do most mornings. I look forward to my daily regime as I have taught myself to enjoy it by using the motivation exercise technique. Years ago I would have found it a drag and quit after the initial enthusiasm had worn off. Nowadays, I am running on a mental programme that tells me I love exercise and the rewards it brings. You too can re-programme your mind in the same way by using the same technique.

Motivation exercise technique – learning to love exercising!

The following self-hypnosis technique will help you to build a strong inner desire to take more exercise and become fitter. Read the script through a few times until you are familiar with the technique. You don't need to learn it word by word as you just need an overview. The key to using the script successfully is to get yourself into a relaxed and receptive state so you absorb the motivation affirmations and visualisations on a deep level. Once you have a grasp of the technique, practise it for the next few days. As with all things, the more you practise, the better you will get at it and the stronger the effects will be.

- Go to a quiet, darkened room where there are no distractions. Take a moment to get into a comfortable position, close your eyes and focus your attention on your breathing. Begin to breathe very slowly and deeply – in through your nose and out through your mouth. Make each breath long and deep, feel your rib cage expand as you breathe in. Continue this for a short while until all the tension disappears from your body and you feel nice and relaxed.

- Continue to breathe slowly and deeply in a steady, rhythmical breathing pattern and, when you reach the top of your breath, hold it for three seconds. Then silently count to five on every out-breath. Continue to relax more and more with every slow out-breath.

- When you feel completely relaxed, I want you to create a visualisation in your mind's eye. Imagine you are participating regularly in exercise in your daily life. Visualise yourself indulging in your exercise routine. This may be working out at the gym, practising yoga, playing tennis, cycling, jogging or whatever you have previously decided is right for you. As you see yourself doing one or more activity, really connect with a feeling of great pleasure and enjoyment. In your mind's eye, really love the feeling the exercise gives you. Make the visualisation clear and use all of your senses to create a realistic mental image.

- Imagine yourself getting great pleasure from the exercise and create a strong feeling that you really want to do it every day. It is important to use your feelings here so that you anchor the feeling of enjoyment into your unconscious mind. Take time to do this and really let your imagination go.

▓ After you have visualised, I want you to repeat the following affirmations to yourself. Say each affirmation ten times or more in a slow, rhythmical way, almost like a slow, steady chant. Say them with real feeling and emotion. Imagine every part of you repeating the affirmations with complete conviction and self-belief, in the present tense. Draw the phrases deep inside you when you say them:

* I love to exercise and keep fit.
* I feel inspired and motivated now.
* I deserve to be fit and healthy.
* I love my fitness workouts.

Feel free to adapt these affirmations to suit your specific aims.

▓ Once you have finished your affirmations, you can compound these new beliefs by using this counting method. Slowly count from one to three and, when you reach the number three, affirm that these positive new beliefs will sink ten times deeper into your unconscious mind, and the positive feelings will grow ten times stronger. When you reach the number three, every cell in your mind, body and spirit will resonate with positive energy. Take a moment to enjoy this feeling and to accept every new belief as a reality.

■ When you are ready to awaken, slowly count from one to ten, open your eyes and you will come back to full waking consciousness.

■ Use this self-hypnosis technique a few times to learn to love exercise and you will never again think of it as a struggle. It becomes something you genuinely enjoy and look forward to doing.

Summary

✓ **Stress-free health** – *believe that you can be fit, healthy and free of illness.*

✓ **Detox your body** – *the quickest and healthiest way to break free of food addictions and lose weight.*

✓ **Healthy eating tips** – *a powerful self-hypnosis technique to help you to eradicate sweets, cakes, chocolate, sugar, coffee or any type of junk food from your diet.*

✓ **A holistic approach to exercise and becoming fit** – *helping you to create a positive exercise plan that suits you.*

✓ **The motivation exercise technique** – *hypnotise yourself to love exercise.*

STEP 6

De-stress your mind

Knowing your own mind

Your mind is an incredibly powerful tool that will help you to achieve many great things. Think of your mind as like a vast computer that you can learn to programme. With a little know-how, you can erase any negative, destructive patterns and programme your mind with positive new beliefs. If you want to develop your physical body shape, you need to put in effort and the same applies to developing a more relaxed and positive mindset. By using the hypnotherapy CD and practising many of the techniques in this book regularly, you will be on the path to achieving this goal and realising your full creative potential.

Einstein said we use only ten per cent of our brain. We are the only species on the planet who do not use our full brain capacity. Every other animal, bird and fish has the use of 100 per cent of their brain. As humans, the largest part of our mind is the unconscious part. Think of this iceberg analogy – the conscious, thinking, analytical part of our mind is the ten per cent of the iceberg above the water, the unconscious part is the 90 per cent submerged below the water. When you close your eyes and relax your mind and body, you are able to tap into your unconscious mind. Self-hypnosis is a very good habit to get into as it can help you get over so many of life's obstacles. The self-hypnosis guide at the end of this book on page 176 can be adapted for many different situations.

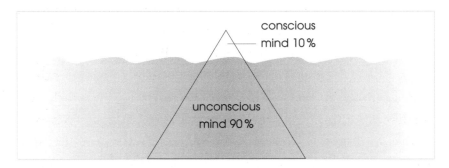

Your unconscious mind is the part where your innermost fears and anxieties reside. It is also where your creativity and talents lie. It then follows that when you tap into this part of your mind, you can rid yourself of fears and draw out the creative genius inside you. Every single one of us has unlimited talents and unique gifts, but more often than not, we do not exploit our potential. This can be because of a lack of belief or simply not understanding how you can access the innate gifts that you possess. We all use the larger unconscious part of our mind but not always automatically. It requires a little discipline to draw out your inner talents. Learning to programme

> 'Perhaps the only limits to the human mind are those we believe in.'
> **Willis Harman**

your mind is a great habit to get into. It will help you to feel much more in control of your feelings and emotions, and become more focused and determined to express your true potential.

Detoxing your mind

If you feel there is a recurring pattern of behaviour that is holding you back, you will need to address this issue before you can move forward. If you have negative patterns holding you back, you need to get to the root cause and rid yourself of the problem first. This will then liberate you and allow your positive programming to be effective with nothing now holding you back. This can be achieved with a little self-analysis and then self-hypnosis. If the problem is deep-rooted and complex, working with a well-qualified hypno-therapist may be the solution. See page 182 for hypnotherapy resources.

When helping my clients get over destructive patterns of behaviour, I always find 'regression to cause' achieves great results. 'Regression to cause' literally means regressing the client under hypnosis, back to the first time their problem began. This is called the seeding incident and this technique works because when we store memories and experiences, we also store the associated emotions as well. So if you experience an emotional trauma or an unpleasant shock of some kind and it is not dealt with or processed through therapy, it will remain unresolved. The negative experience then becomes repressed along with the negative emotions. Sometimes these memories, particularly if experienced in childhood, become consciously forgotten but they still lurk around in your subconscious mind. If something triggers that memory years later, the emotions are also released. This is called the secondary incident and when this occurs, it can cause you to overreact to situations in a negative way or to sabotage things that you want to achieve. This can be very confusing if you do not understand *why* you react in this way.

There is always a reason behind our idiosyncratic patterns of behaviour. We are all conditioned by events that have occurred in our pasts, more so than many people realise. Your habits and the way you react to situations often come from blueprint experiences in your formative years. If a trauma occurs in your infancy or childhood, the feeling it creates in you will be stored for future reference. For example, if a small child sees their mother scream and panic every time she sees a spider, the mother is indirectly teaching her child that spiders are something to be feared. This learned pattern of behaviour becomes rooted in the unconscious mind of the child. I once treated a client who only ever had panic attacks when she went on holiday. After regressing her to the cause of the problem, it came to light that the preparations for her childhood family holidays were always very stressful. As an adult she had an unconscious programme confirming that going on holiday creates anxiety. This is an example of how our childhood experiences can affect us in so many different ways.

Failure to recognise negative conditioned patterns is something that holds most people back in life. It is not always easy getting over negative conditioning. It is often multi-layered and unravelling it can be likened to peeling away the layers of an onion. You can overcome one issue, only to find another layer below. However, the more work you do in this area, the more liberated you become.

When de-stressing your life, one of the most important things you can do is to rid yourself of destructive patterns of behaviour. That is, unless you had an idyllic, stress-free upbringing with two loving parents who always made you feel secure, nurtured you through every stage of your development and instilled in you a great self-belief. If only!

Reframing problems

Feeling stressed is all in the mind. When you feel stressed, you are reacting to a situation. Sometimes you react to a situation out of habit, as discussed in the previous paragraphs. When you learn to temper the way you react to problems, you will have more control of your stress levels. The following is a de-stress technique to help you to cope with an unexpected stressful problem as it arises.

De-stress technique – reframing stressful situations

- The next time something happens to cause you stress, ask yourself if this will matter in one month's time. More often than not, it will not mean a thing to you. Think back to things that stressed you in the past month or so and you'll find that most of them were insignificant and caused you no lasting problem. It's often the way we react that exacerbates the stress we feel. So, as well as asking yourself if it will matter in one month, clear your mind, breathe slowly and deeply and count to ten. Then allow yourself to evaluate the situation again.

When you are faced with an unexpected problem, always tackle it as it arises. Try not to react immediately, but rather take time to reframe the situation. Are there any positives to be learnt from the problem? What can it teach you? Above all, be proactive and deal with it in the best way you can.

Another way to reframe a problem is to look at it from another perspective. Imagine you are viewing the problem from a distance, as though you are outside yourself and have an objective view of the whole picture. You can imagine you are looking at it from above. This helps you to emotionally disassociate from the problem and is a good way to deal with problems that cause you emotional anxiety.

It can sometimes help to turn to others when problems mount up. When we get caught up in the middle of a problem we can't always see the wood for the trees. It can sometimes help to get some outside wisdom and insight from others who have your best interests at heart. If there is someone you know who handles pressure and adversity well, ask yourself how this person would resolve your dilemma. Think of someone who has qualities that you admire and use them as an inspiration and imagine yourself handling the problem in the same way that they would. The following is a brief NLP (Neuro-Linguistic Programming) modelling technique. It is a therapeutic tool for effective communication, goal-setting, influencing, accelerated learning and changing behaviour patterns. It will help you draw from other people's positive examples of coping with stress and then import these characteristics into your consciousness.

De-stress technique – the modelling technique

- Close your eyes and centre your mind through your deep breathing. When your mind is calm and clear, focus your thoughts on someone whom you admire. Think of a person who has real character and strength, and is good at dealing with problems and pressure. Take a moment to see this person in your mind's eye and focus on their qualities.

- Imagine that all of these characteristics are becoming part of you. Feel as though you are drawing these positive traits deep inside yourself. Whatever it is that you admire in this person, imagine you are absorbing and assimilating these qualities. Maybe it is their strength in adversity or their composure when dealing with problems?

- Now visualise yourself expressing these positive traits with the same confidence and self-belief. Take a moment to focus on this. Be creative and use all of your senses when you visualise yourself expressing these new, positive characteristics.

You can adapt this technique for many different purposes. For example, if you want to be able to achieve an adventurous goal that is outside your comfort zone, model yourself on someone who is bold and thrives on challenges. Be creative when you use these techniques and adapt them for your specific needs.

Time management

As I said at the beginning of this book, for most people life has never been busier. Nowadays life moves at 100 miles per hour and so much of it is fast and furious. We often

> 'What may be done at any time will be done at no time.'
> **Scottish proverb**

demand quick fixes and instant solutions and have many decisions to make in an average week. This busy, demanding pace of life can be a big cause of stress. To counter-balance dealing with the pressures of modern-day life, you need to manage your time effectively. This can mean avoiding pro-crastinating and dealing with things as they arise, rather than allowing the pressures of uncompleted tasks to build and build.

De-stress tip – getting things done

- Each morning, get into the habit of dealing with every-thing that arrives in the mail or by email straight away. Make the phone calls you need to make and reply to everything immediately. Prioritise their importance and work through all your tasks systematically. Being more proactive and efficient in this way will help you feel more in control of your affairs. It will feel good to get into the habit of using your time effectively.

The positive side to life in the twenty-first century is that we generally have more freedom and control of our lives when we manage our time well. One way to manage your time more effectively is to make a habit of focusing on the most important things in your life. Regularly evaluate how you can use your time in the best possible way. Ask yourself what are your goals and objectives, what do you want to achieve in the short term and long term? Introducing more structure and planning into your life – to your work, home and social life – will make you feel more organised and therefore less stressed.

Whenever something is not working in your life, let it go. Never be afraid to say 'no' to people. Sometimes other people can be a drain on our time and energy, and most good-natured people can find it hard to be honest and say 'no'. However, it is very liberating. Avoid being a pleaser all the time. Think of it this way: when someone is a pushover, other people lose respect for them. If you are forever saying 'yes' and doing things for other people when you don't really want to, people will take advantage of you. It is human nature. They may be grateful for your deeds but they will not really respect you in spite of what they may say. So the next time someone asks you to do something you don't really want to do, give them a polite and respectful 'no'. I have to do this a lot in my work because sometimes my workload gets very heavy, but I have learnt to delegate and, if I can't help some-one, I always try to refer them on to someone who I think can. Remember, the vast majority of people will not think any less of you if say, 'Sorry, I haven't got time' or 'I've already got something booked'.

De-stress technique – saying 'no' to people

■ If you find it hard to say 'no' to people and you have a specific situation where you would like to do this but find it difficult, visualising it beforehand can help. Close your eyes and create the scene with the person you want to be honest with. Imagine the picture in detail and see yourself expressing your point of view very clearly and confidently and saying exactly what you want to say. Imagine this visualisation a few times and it will help you to find the courage to speak your truth when you are in the real situation.

The following time management tips will help you feel more organised and in control of your time.

Time management – top ten tips

1) Be proactive and deal with problems and tasks as they arise. When problems or dilemmas arrive by post in the morning, or by email or fax, address them straight away. By not procrastinating and dealing with things straight away, you will minimise the stressful effects.

2) Get rid of time-wasting habits or patterns. For example, if you have regular meetings or commitments that are unfulfilling or you feel achieve little, get rid of them from your schedule. Or maybe, if it's shopping that takes up too much of your time, look at the option of shopping online. Don't be afraid to make changes if you need to give yourself more time for the more important and fulfilling things in life.

3) When you are busy, limit the time spent on uncreative leisure habits, like watching TV, net surfing and emailing, or long personal calls that are not essential.

4)   Regularly evaluate how you use your time most effect-
      ively. Prioritise and then plan how you can make the
      best use of your time. Keep a large diary with each day
      on a single page and list in it all the things you will do in
      the following week. Start with the most important things
      first and then fill in the spaces with the less important
      tasks. Make sure to include plenty of rest and relaxation
      activities in your schedule. As you finish each task, tick
      it in your diary and feel how satisfying that tick is!

5)   Learn to say 'no' to people and don't try to please every-
      one all the time. Use the de-stress visualisation technique
      above to help you in this area.

6)   Avoid trying to do too much – it can be as stressful
      as doing too little. Do as much as you can and then
      switch off.

7)   Always delegate whenever possible. If you can't do it,
      recommend someone else who can.

8)   If you feel overworked or stressed, make time for rest
      and relaxation. Twenty or thirty minutes of self-hypnosis
      or meditation are great ways to clear your head and
      recharge. You will always be able to work more produc-
      tively after relaxing your mind and body. When you do
      this, you will feel mentally and physically refreshed when
      you begin working again.

9)   The best way to absorb information when you are study-
      ing or learning is to work for twenty minutes, then take
      two minutes off to quiet the mind and assimilate the

knowledge. The brain stores and absorbs the information more easily this way.

10) Accept that there are only twenty-four hours in a day and you can only do so much. If you work hard, never berate yourself for not doing enough. Make sure you get your work and life balance right. If everything gets on top of you, go for a walk in nature and take stock of everything from a distance. Imagine you are above yourself looking down on your life and all the day-to-day events. When you do this, detach yourself from any emotional problems or dilemmas. Regularly step away from things and view your life from a higher perspective.

De-stress your memory

Having a bad memory can be a cause of stress, causing life to be disorganised and untidy. The good news is that your memory is like a muscle and, with practise, it can improve, even with age. It is a myth that memory deteriorates with age. Every year there is a memory Olympics where people pit their memory skills against each other for prizes and awards. Some of the memory feats on display are astounding. The one thing these memory champions all have in common is that their skills are learnt. They are not blessed with super-natural memory talents; they simply train their minds to remember sequences of information. That means you and I can do the same and develop brilliant memories if we put in the effort.

While most of us don't want to become memory champions, it is always handy to learn a few techniques to help us sharpen and improve our memory skills. The first thing you must never do is to tell yourself you have a bad memory – this is a golden rule. So many people believe their memory will worsen with age and it becomes a mantra that they repeat over and over to themselves and others. This is an affirmation and, if you say it often enough, it becomes self-fulfilling. Just because you lose your car keys or forget a birthday doesn't mean you have a bad memory. It just means your focus was elsewhere. So get rid of any belief that your memory will deteriorate with age and accept that from now on, your memory is going to improve.

De-stress technique – never forget a name ever again

- Here is a simple technique you can use to remember the names of people you meet. The next time you meet someone whose name you want to remember, link their first and last names to famous names. For example, you meet a man called John Marley. Close your eyes and visualise him in a scene with John Lennon and Bob Marley. Maybe imagine your new acquaintance on stage jamming away with John and Bob? Create a clear picture in your mind of the three of them together. The more colourful the image the better, and use as many senses as you can when creating the visualisation. Reinforce the image a few times and it will become very strong and create a permanent, long-term memory.

When you practise visualisations like this, the memory will be long-lasting. This is because the mind stores and recalls visual images more easily than words. Years ago I taught my son some visualisation techniques to help him to remember many of the Japanese words he needed to recall for his judo exam. He still remembers many of those unusual sounding words today, even though he has not thought about them for years. This is because whenever he thinks about his judo exam, the pictures he associated with the words begin to drift back into his awareness. Once the pictures are in his head, the associated words follow. We all have an unlimited storage capacity in our minds when we use visualisation techniques. It is these methods that enable those memory champions to achieve their amazing feats.

There are many people who are banned from casinos because of their ability to counts cards. They can memorise the cards that get dealt and therefore have a better idea of which cards are still left in the pack. This tilts the chances of winning in their favour and gives them an edge over the casino. Most casinos naturally prefer the advantage to be the other way around. Being an ace card counter is an example of just one of the many perks of having a superb memory, but you will also need to be good at creating disguises to have a lasting career in this area! Seriously, there are many techniques you can learn to improve your memory, which can be a great help when studying for exams, learning new languages or when you perform any task that requires you to store and recall information. There are many books and CDs that can help you to develop your memory skills. If this is an area you would like to explore further, there are some references on page 181.

How to store and recall information effectively

When you are faced with a heavy workload and you have to take in a lot of information, you will need strategies to help you. It can also help to know yourself a little better, as we all absorb information differently. Everyone has a dominant sense. For most people, their visual sense is their primary conduit for absorbing information. For some, it can be kinaesthetic (feeling), audible, taste or smell. To find out which of the five senses is your dominant one, ask yourself the following questions: do you often think and remember in pictures or do you recall information more easily through your feelings? If old songs easily trigger a barrage of memories, then maybe your dominant sense is through your hearing. Look beyond the obvious and be your own therapist here. Your language patterns can sometimes give you clues. Do you often use phrases like, 'I'm feeling fine' or 'I hear what you say' or 'I can see what you mean'? Look at any common patterns in your ways of communication for clues to your dominant sense. Close your eyes now and take a minute to figure out the sense you use most frequently to store and recall information.

Once you know which is your dominant sense, this can help you in the future. You can give priority to this sense whenever you want to remember some information. For example, imagine you are studying for an upcoming test and you want to visualise your exam day. Your aim is to be alert and focused on the day of the exam and also to recall everything you have learnt. So, you would relax and visualise yourself in the exam room. If your preferred sense was kinaesthetic, you could create a trigger by affirming that as you feel the pen in your hand, your mind will become sharp and alert and you will be in complete control of your feelings. This is called an anchor. You create visualisations, positive thoughts, affirmations and feelings and anchor them to a future situation. When you sit the exam for real, the feeling of the pen in your hand will act as a trigger for you, and you will create a peak performance state just when you need it when the pressure is on. Most top athletes use techniques like this when they need to be at their very best. It gives them a psychological edge. Being able to focus the mind and achieve a peak performance state when competing is crucial in top-level sport.

The secret ingredient for creating effective visualisations is compounding: the more you repeat a visualisation in your mind, the stronger it will become. This is because when you visualise, your unconscious mind doesn't distinguish between what is real and imagined. So when you regularly visualise yourself in a future situation performing wonderfully well, your unconscious mind accepts this as a reality. It doesn't know that you are simply imagining it; it believes you are actually doing it now. When the big day actually arrives and you need to be at your best, your mind will be well conditioned. It will accept that you perform well in this situation and respond accordingly. Use the guide to self-hypnosis on page 176 to help you achieve a peak performance state any time you need to. Remember that your visualisations will always be more effective when you use all of your senses to absorb images.

De-stress tip – the effective learning method

- Whenever you are reading, studying or learning something new, the optimum way to absorb information is twenty minutes on, followed by two minutes off. Study for twenty minutes then clear your mind for two, then begin again. Use the two minutes for deep breathing and stilling your mind. This cycle allows your brain to take in and assimilate smaller chunks of information, rather than being overloaded by a mass of information.

Mind-calming and body relaxation technique

- Close your eyes and practise your preferred slow, deep breathing technique, which you will be familiar with by now. Allow your mind to go completely blank. Don't worry if you still get unwanted thoughts drifting into your mind; tell yourself not to fight them as they will soon drift away again. Every time you get an unwanted thought, imagine a large red stop sign. As soon as you see the red stop sign, imagine the thought disappearing and your mind becoming clear.

- Another thought-clearing technique is to imagine a large computer screen full of data that becomes blank by hitting a keypad. Imagine that by pressing a keypad you can clear your mind. Or imagine you are looking up at the sky on a pleasant summer's day. You notice a few small clouds that drift across the sky and then fade away.

Eventually all of the clouds have drifted away and the sky is clear. Imagine your conscious thoughts are like clouds that fade away. Use whatever method works best for you.

■ Now you can relax your body. Imagine every muscle from the top of your head to the tips of your toes completely relaxing. You can start at the top and systematically work your way down to your toes. Imagine your eyelids have become heavy and tired and any tension in your fore-head is disappearing. All the muscles there are becom-ing loose and relaxed.

■ Continue this pattern and imagine all the muscles relaxing in your jaw, neck, shoulders, back, arms and legs. Imagine the relaxation spreading down through your body, letting go of any tightness or tension in all your muscles. You can visualise the muscles relaxing and spend extra time relaxing any part of your body that holds more tension. Allow the outside world to fade into the back-ground and continue your journey into your inner world.

■ When you have finished your body relaxation and you are completely relaxed from head to toe, you can repeat the following affirmations. When you do so, imagine every part of you absorbing the affirmations with real feeling and emotion so that every cell in your mind and body resonates with each phrase.

* I am at peace with myself and the world around me.
* I feel centred and balanced.
* My mind is calm and clear.
* I feel calm and composed under pressure.

■ When you are ready to awaken, slowly count from one to ten, open your eyes and come back to full waking consciousness.

Summary

✓ **Knowing your own mind** – *understanding how your mind works.*

✓ **Detoxing your mind** – *getting rid of old destructive patterns of behaviour and replacing them with new positive ones.*

✓ **Reframing problems** – *overcoming problems by approaching them in positive new ways.*

✓ **Time management** - *tips and techniques to help you manage your time more effectively.*

✓ **De-stress your memory** – *reframing your beliefs about your memory, plus tips and resources to develop a stronger memory.*

✓ **How to store and recall information effectively** – *tips and techniques to help you with studying and memory in general.*

✓ **Mind-calming and body relaxation technique** – *a self-hypnosis technique to calm your mind and relax your body.*

STEP 7

De-stress your future

Developing a positive outlook

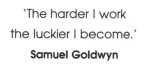

Feeling insecure about the future can be a cause of stress. When people get stuck in a rut and have a bleak view of the future, it can lead to apathy and induce feelings of anxiety. However, with a little effort, it is easy to create a more positive outlook. Your future can be as bright as you want it to be. If you believe that you are destined to have abundant health, happiness and prosperity then that is what you will create. Conversely, if you are insecure about the future and feel the outlook is bleak then this will again become self-fulfilling. You will unconsciously create situations that mirror your innermost beliefs. The things you do now will go towards creating your future. So developing a positive outlook is very important.

'The harder I work the luckier I become.'
Samuel Goldwyn

The power of positive thinking is nothing new. It is something many ancient cultures believed in and embraced. 'He who can believe himself well will be well.' This is a 2,000-year-old quote from a Roman poet called Ovid. He believed in the mind's unlimited ability to transform and heal, and so should we all. Even when your circumstances are not congruent with the lifestyle you believe you deserve, never doubt your ability to make positive changes. You need to start with the way you think and adopt the 'fake it until you make it' principle. That is, to continually affirm and enforce the belief that your future is golden. When you do this, you will attract opportunities towards you and you will find you become 'luckier'. The two main ways you create a positive outlook are on a conscious level through affirmation and on an unconscious level through self-hypnosis. The positive future visualisation technique at the end of this chapter, along with the CD, will help you do this.

De-stress tip – create the belief first, then the reality will follow.

■　To create a positive future, you have to believe your future is golden in the first place. Even if things are not how you want them to be now, you can always change your future. You do this not through hoping, wishing or yearning, which is weak and ineffective, but through positive visualisation and creating strong inner beliefs that your future will be everything you want it to be.

Embracing the ageing process

Many people are fearful of getting older, especially in our generation, where youth and physical perfection assume such importance in the media. More and more people try to turn back the clock in increasingly drastic ways. We have all seen the horror shows where people have had too much surgery and end up looking freaky. Anti-ageing treatments like cosmetic surgery and botox are becoming increasingly common. The ageing process, which should be embraced as a natural part of life, is something that causes many people stress. Some become more fearful and even reclusive with age. It doesn't help that the elderly are not respected in the way that they should be. Many cultures, quite logically, hold their elders in high esteem, but in the West we have lost this tradition.

People also worry about their health as they age and don't realise they have the power to make positive changes towards becoming healthier. The older generations have been indoctrinated into believing that modern medicine has most of the answers. This is not true. Modern medicine only treats symptoms, it doesn't cure disease. A healthy sugar- and additive-free organic diet, along with regular exercise, will prevent the onset of almost all illness and disease. It really is that simple. But then life *is* simple when you get it right. So keep working on achieving that simplicity through making as many small positive changes as you can.

If ageing and health are concerns for you, you need to stop worrying and be proactive. If you work on your health through diet and exercise, you will slow the ageing process. There are zillions of anti-ageing products on the market but without a doubt, the best remedy is a very healthy diet. There is nothing wrong with creams and potions, but start with diet and exercise first. Regular, healthy sleep will also help you to look younger than your years. When I was twenty, I could spend the weekend boozing, smoking and partying all night and still wake up on Monday morning looking like an airbrushed rock star. If I carried on like that now, I'd look like a bloated old vagrant in no time! It is a fact of life that you have to work a little harder to remain vibrant and healthy as you get older. But you can enjoy doing just that through your visualisations. When you create a healthy holistic lifestyle it can become a little addictive. A positive addiction like that is fine, as long as it is not extreme.

There is nothing wrong with wanting to slow the ageing process a little, but try to keep it in balance. Don't obsess about ageing or get down about the way your face and body changes as you grow older. It happens to everyone, the poor, the rich and the famous. Having a positive attitude will help you to adapt to changes in your life. When you learn to accept that the ageing process is a natural part of life, growing old is not a stressful concept.

If you have a problem accepting the way you look, the following technique will help. It may not be easy at first, as you are trying to change your perception and create a more positive feeling of self-acceptance. The way to approach this is to view it as though you are re-programming your mind to feel more positive about yourself. They say there are three perceptions of one's self: our own, other people's and the real one. If you feel better about yourself and the way you look, your self-perception will become more positive. This in itself will make you come across as a more positive person and, as a result,

> 'He who is of calm and happy nature will hardly feel the pressure of age, but to him who is of an opposite disposition youth and age are equally a burden.'
> **Plato**

you will also appear more attractive to others. When using this technique, use the 'fake it until you make it' principle, even if it feels awkward at first. If you can scale the heights and love yourself unconditionally, other people will become more loving towards you. Whatever the 'inner you' projects outwards will affect the way people respond to you.

De-stress technique – accepting yourself and the way you look

- Go to a quiet room and look at your face in the mirror. Look at your face closely and accept yourself as you are with any lines or imperfections. Take a few deep breaths and relax and clear your mind of any conscious thought. Aim to create a feeling of complete relaxation through your breathing and mental focus. Then project a strong feeling of love and acceptance as you stare at your face and into your eyes. Repeat to yourself, 'I love and accept myself'. Again, use your feelings. Project a feeling of love, compassion and acceptance for who you are and the way you look. Make the feelings very positive and continue this habit on a daily basis.

The above technique has a broader application than just feeling more positive about the way you look. It can also enhance your self-esteem and confidence. If you want to work on your self-image a little more, you can combine this with the following technique. Once again, you are aiming to programme your mind with a new belief, which it will then automatically respond to.

De-stress technique II – developing your self-confidence

■ Close your eyes and relax. Then imagine yourself as you want to be. See a picture of the perfect you standing in front of you, full of confidence and self-belief. See the confident way this self-assured you stands and how you hold yourself. Make the picture very positive and bright and clear.

■ Now step into your perfect self as though you are looking out through your own eyes. Notice how good you feel. Amplify the positive feelings and affirm they will stay with you in your every day life.

Practise both techniques regularly, especially at times when you need a boost of confidence and self-esteem.

Setting goals for your future

You would not get on a bus if you did not know where it was going, so apply this principle to your life. Do you have a clear idea of what you want from your life, both personally and in your work? Making plans for your future and having clear aims in life is important. When you have goals and things to aim for, it gives you a sense of purpose and direction. It also helps to give you a positive outlook.

Take a moment now to write down a list of goals. Have one list of goals for your personal life and one for your work or career. List a minimum of ten clear goals for each. Remember to write your goals and affirmations in the present tense, as though they are a reality now. When making your lists, make sure you set a time frame for all the goals to be achieved. Head your list by stating: Goals I will achieve by (date here).

Here are some examples of personal goals that may give you ideas for your list. **The first sentence clarifies your goal,** and the following sentence should affirm what you want to achieve from your goal.

- **I am learning to play the guitar (or any musical instrument).** I love practising the guitar and learning new techniques.

- **I am learning to play golf/tennis/badminton (or any sport that takes your fancy).** I get great enjoyment from playing _____

- **I am learning a new language.** I love the challenge of learning this new language and feel determined to achieve a higher level of fluency.

- **I am a master in the art of meditation.** I enjoy meditating every day as it brings me inner peace and wisdom.

- **I practise yoga every day**. I love learning about and practising yoga as it brings me peace and calm and gives me more energy.

- **I have stopped smoking forever.** I am now a non-smoker and I love being free of the burden of smoking.

■ **I have achieved my ideal target weight.** Your weight goal should always be clarified by the amount of weight you aim to lose and the time frame. For example, I will achieve my target weight of ten stone by the (date).

LIST OF PERSONAL GOALS

These are just examples of personal goals. When you make your lists, write down as many as you can and make sure to set the future date. Do not limit your lists – the more goals you have the better. You may not achieve them all in the time frame, but you will achieve many of them. You should revise and update your goals every six or twelve months. When you write them down, make sure they are things you genuinely want to achieve or have an interest in. Think of why you want to achieve them and what purpose they will serve in your life. There is no point in going back to college to study for an

English degree if you are not going to do anything with it. So think your goals through carefully and look at how they will serve you.

Here are some examples of some work and career goals.

- **I am self-employed.** I love to work for myself as it gives me a wonderful sense of freedom.

- **I have my dream job working for** _____ I love working for this company and in this industry as I have great interest in this area.

- **I earn a salary of £100,000 per year in my dream job.**

- **I am head of my new department.**

- **I own my own thriving business.**

LIST OF WORK AND CAREER GOALS

_____

_____

_____

_____

_____

_____

_____

_____

_____

_____

It is important to set high ceilings for your goals. Even if they initially seem out of reach, do not put a limitation on what you can achieve. When I first started setting my goals, I found that I would sometimes write them down enthusiastically and then have a few self-doubts creep in. But I persevered and worked on getting rid of any self-doubts or limiting beliefs. One of my goals was to sell 100,000 copies of my hypnosis tapes within three years. I remember looking at this goal and thinking, wouldn't that be great, but a part of me didn't really believe it was possible as a self-published one-man-band. I was recording my tapes on a home recording set-up in a back bedroom in my tiny, two-bedroom terraced house. I then duplicated the cassettes one at a time and printed the covers on my home printer. I made displays for them from wood that I bought from B&Q and sold the tapes into a few local shops.

I worked hard on my affirmations and getting rid of any doubts or limiting beliefs and within two years, I had made that target and sold 100,000 tapes. It felt really good to know that I could be the master my own destiny. It made me realise I had the ability to change my life through my own focused efforts. The momentum of that first affirmation and clear statement of intent has carried the project further than I could have imagined. The beauty of this kind of work is that when you create goals and you succeed in achieving them, your belief in what you can achieve in the future becomes stronger. At first it feels like you are turning the tide and things happen slowly, but, as your energy grows, you can manifest things much more quickly and easily. A few months ago I decided I wanted to sell lots of my books but needed a major book publishing deal to make this happen. I put the affirmation out there and started on my goal without a doubt it would materialise. I asked two of the ladies who work for me to call a few agents from the *Writers' and Artists' Yearbook* and arrange some appointments. After an hour they came back with the despondent response that they could not get past the receptionists at the agencies. Every call they made was greeted with a standard response to send in the manuscript.

So I tried myself. I picked out an agency from the book. I made the call and managed to get past the receptionist only to be put through to the wrong department and an answering machine. I left a message espousing the sales success of my tape and CDs and explaining what I wanted. A week later an agent called me back expressing some interest. He had been walking past the office as someone was playing the message and he thought it sounded interesting. We met in London and got on well. He is a down-to-earth guy and we found we had similar backgrounds and shared similar interests. To cut a long story short, within a few short weeks my agent had helped me to secure a six-figure, three-book deal with one of the UK's biggest publishers. The deal happened so quickly, I think, because I never doubted it would happen. I believed I was in the right place at the right time and the universe delivered this back to me. They call it 'cosmic ordering' these days.

Set your goals sky-high, put energy into them and continually revise them year after year. You will be amazed at what you can achieve when you become single-minded and create a strong momentum.

Express yourself through effective communication

When you communicate, get in the habit of expressing yourself clearly. When others know where you are coming from, they will respond accordingly. If you are clear and unambiguous when you communicate, people will understand you. Get in the habit of speaking your mind and being truthful. Even if people don't agree with you, an honest approach will always gain respect. You should always speak up for yourself and say your truth. If you are in a dispute or need to negotiate, always start off in a positive way so that you avoid further conflict. Starting with a compliment and pleasant small talk is always a good opening gambit. When you begin on positive terms, it is easier to get your point across and be understood.

De-stress technique – communicating effectively

■ When you want to communicate more effectively in a future situation, visualising it beforehand will help you on many levels. If you want to impress on a date, make a good speech or just feel more relaxed in a social setting, visualising it will help prepare you in the best possible way. So go somewhere quiet where you won't be disturbed, close your eyes and breathe slowly and deeply. Allow yourself to relax and clear your mind of all thought.

■ Once you are pleasantly relaxed, imagine the future situation in your mind's eye. See yourself communicating clearly and effectively. If you are on a date or in a light-hearted social setting, see yourself laughing with people and having great fun. If it is a meeting, see yourself getting your point across clearly and respectfully. Whatever the situation, accentuate the positives and make the picture as big and bright as you can. Use all of your senses to enhance the image and let your imagination go. The more positive the image, the more powerful the after-effects will be.

■ Repeat the technique as often as you can so that it becomes a strong inner belief. If you use it for lots of different situations where you need to communicate, you will soon become a very skilled and effective communicator. I was once terrified of public speaking, but nowadays I use this technique whenever I do a talk or presentation and it helps me every time.

When communicating with others, make a habit of being generous with your words. Words are free and it will cost you nothing to give compliments or praise. Many people feel insecure and, when you give others a simple compliment, it can make a big difference to how they feel. It will also help you to feel big-hearted and good about yourself. It is good to express yourself in a positive way by saying something nice to others in the form of compliments or praise. I have to work at this one as I was part of a south London family that excelled in merciless mickey-taking! I don't think we ever praised each other unless it was a back-handed compliment. If I give someone praise, I sometimes feel I am being insincere or wonder if they think I am being sarcastic. But I am aware that this is just my old programming and something that I work on.

Laughter is a wonderful way to communicate. Laughing and joking with people is a great way to build rapport. People like to be around others who are fun and make them laugh. If there is not enough fun and laughter in your life, work on this consciously. Develop the art of being light-hearted and having fun. You only have to look at children to re-learn how to do this. Children know instinctively how to play and have fun. Unfortunately, life can knock this out of us when we become adults. Life can be too serious with all the doom and gloom in the world and the many responsibilities we have to face. Many adults have simply lost the use of their chuckle muscle! That is the ability to be fun and light-hearted. If you have kids, then they will help you to have fun if you encourage them and give them your time.

When my son was growing up, I loved nothing more than taking him and his mates to the park and playing football with them. I think I enjoyed it more than they did because it re-connected me back to the kid in me. It is very liberating to connect with this child part of yourself now and again. Practise the habit of having fun and being carefree. Do something every day that is spontaneous and even childlike. Having fun is infectious and will lift your mood and that of others around you.

De-stress technique – connecting with
your carefree self

■ Close your eyes and think of a time when something happened that made you laugh a lot. Maybe you were with a friend and something tickled you. Remember that time and reconnect with the feelings. When you remember the happy event, all the positive emotions that are stored with the memory will come back to you and lift your mood.

Building your self-esteem

As the song goes, if you don't love and respect yourself, then no one else will. When you love yourself in a non-egotistical way, it will shine through and make you more attractive. People are drawn to others who have an inner calmness and serenity about them. If you weren't taught to love and respect yourself, you will need to work on it. The first rule is to banish negative self-talk from your vocabulary. I mentioned earlier in the book that self-criticism is very destructive. If you are forever berating yourself for being stupid or foolish, this will become self-fulfilling. You should never again speak negatively to yourself because all you are doing is programming yourself to feel bad.

After banishing self-criticism from your inner dialogue, you can learn to love yourself by focusing on your successes. On one of my early hypnosis tapes, I instructed the listener to do just that, to focus on their successes in life however great or small. I was amazed by the calls and emails from people saying they couldn't get on with that particular tape, as they had never had any success in their lives. It seemed many people could not see any success in their life but, after speaking with them, I would always find many successes. I had to rework that title and get the same point across in a different way.

Being a good parent to your children is a huge success in life and very underrated. Being kind, loving, compassionate and generous are also successful traits that most people possess. If you have ever won or achieved anything, however small, don't be afraid to praise yourself. British people are not encouraged to love and respect themselves. This is a bit of a generalisation, but many Brits will know what I mean. We grow up believing that we must play down our achievements. I disagree. I think you should celebrate every little success you have in life. Not so you brag or bore people, you can still be humble and modest. Just don't be afraid of praising yourself when you do something well. There is nothing wrong with being pleased and proud of yourself – it should become something you embrace.

> 'It's never too late to be what you might have been.'
> **George Elliot**

De-stress technique – love and respect yourself

- Learn to love yourself completely, faults and all. When you truly love and respect yourself, you open yourself up to being loved and respected by others. Avoid being vain or egotistical, just cultivate the habit of loving yourself by acknowledging your achievements and focusing on your good points. Every one of your achievements must be acknowledged, however great or small. Maybe you are doing well at work, or you have good friendships, or you are a good parent or a good son or daughter. Always look at what you have achieved, acknowledge it and be proud of it.

■ Close your eyes, take a few deep breaths and relax. Clear away any unwanted thoughts and let your mind become still. Take a few moments to do this. Then focus on all the little things that you have achieved in your life; any good work you have done, any good friendships you have cultivated, anything you have won or been praised for. Keep your focus on all the positives in your life and feel good about yourself as you do so. Enhance all the feelings and images by making them big and bright and very clear. Be proud of yourself as you do this and state the affirmations, 'I love and respect myself' and 'I feel proud of myself'. Continue this technique regularly over a number of days until you feel your self-esteem growing stronger.

■ You can also use the accepting yourself technique on page 149 when focusing on your achievements and successes.

> 'Always aim at complete harmony of thought and word and deed. Always aim at purifying your thoughts and everything will be well.
> **Mahatma Gandhi**

When you truly learn to love yourself, you will build an inner energy and power. Outside criticism will not affect you in a negative way. If anyone knocks you or pulls you down, you will find it easy to rise above their criticism. People who are very critical of others are normally insecure themselves; they want to deflect away from their own weaknesses. So never take criticism to heart, just see it for what it is and rise above it. As your self-respect grows stronger, you will find you only attract positive people into your life and you will naturally move away from negative energy-draining types.

Positive future visualisation technique

- Go to a quiet, darkened room where there are no distractions. Close your eyes and focus your attention on your breathing technique. Allow your mind and body to relax.

- Once you are deeply relaxed and your mind is still, tell yourself silently that you are going to visualise your future. Then imagine going forward in time, into your future. Go forward two years in time. Stay deeply relaxed and focus on this, your future, two years from now.

- When you go forward to this future date, visualise your life exactly how you want it to be. See yourself looking fit, healthy and happy and achieving all the things you want to achieve. Use all of your senses to make this a reality. Make it clear how good you look and feel. Use some creative licence to make everything as positive and happy as possible.

- Now accept on every level that this is what you deserve. This is the life that you deserve. Affirm to yourself silently or out loud:

  * I deserve to be happy and healthy.

- Accept this belief unconditionally. Take a moment to enjoy the scenario. As you do so, the feelings and images will sink deeply into your unconscious mind and become a part of your inner reality. Your unconscious mind will then accept your ideal future as real. In your daily life you will unconsciously gravitate towards this happy future.

■ When you are ready to awaken, slowly count from one to ten, open your eyes and come back to full waking consciousness.

■ This future visualisation technique will help you work towards a healthy, happy, positive future on an unconscious level. This means you will become more intuitive and automatically make more good decisions than bad on your journey through life. Creating a profoundly positive belief about your future on a deep, unconscious level can help you in many subtle ways. There is a universal law that states that what you project out will come back to you. So always be very clear and concise when affirming and visualising – you will always get back exactly what you ask for.

Summary

Developing a positive outlook

Embracing the ageing process

Setting your goals for your future

Express yourself through effective communication

Building your self-esteem – *love and respect yourself*

Positive future visualisation technique – *create the future you deserve.*

Finally

I hope that this book has given you inspiration and a few new pointers to help you cope with stress. There is no panacea to cure stress as a whole but, by adopting many of these tips and techniques, you will be able to deal with many of life's problems with a new calmness and composure. Life can be challenging and difficult at times, but it is all about your ability to cope. How you face difficulties will be the making of you. If you learn to rise to challenges and view difficulties as opportunities to learn, you become stronger. Challenge yourself regularly and live your life with courage and confidence. My mother-in-law is eighty-three and she wants to do a parachute jump. She is serious about it and I am one of her few supporters. I think she is making a wonderful positive statement by doing this. When her time is up, she will be remembered for her courage and her positive attitude to life. When your time is up, how do you want to be remembered? Think about that regularly and set your goals high. When you cultivate a positive outlook and aspire to the belief that you can achieve anything, there will not be much in life that phases you.

Follow these rules in life and you won't go far wrong:

■ **Keep things simple and don't get bogged down in trivialities.**

- Develop your self-belief and be respectful to others.

- Always speak your mind.

- Don't lean on others or be needy.

- Banish negative self-talk and avoid negative people at all times.

- Be generous with your words and cultivate a positive outlook.

- Work hard to achieve your goals and always look for new challenges and adventures.

- Avoid reading newspapers or watching fearful or negative TV as much as possible.

- Have new ideas every day, read inspiring books and watch positive, feel-good films.

- Work on your fitness and health, meditate regularly and say your positive affirmations daily.

- Laugh a lot and cultivate the habit of being light-hearted and easy-going.

- Have fun and do things that make you happy.

- Be carefree, different and spontaneous and enjoy making others happy.

- Be big-hearted and generous with your time and money.

- Be loving and compassionate towards all things.

- Love and respect yourself.

- **Be thankful for each new day and wake up every day thinking about what you are going to achieve and how you are going to have fun achieving it.**

- **Live each day to the full.**

These rules of life will keep you on a positive path. Create your own lists, write them down and put them in places where you can read them each day. Make a point of working on one or more of your positive rules each day. Staying on a positive path is the key to a stress-free and happy life. Remember that on an energy level you will attract towards yourself what you give out. You will naturally surround yourself with other positive people and life will become more positive all the time.

> 'Courage is the mastery of fear, not the absence of fear.'
> **Mark Twain**

So make sure you are always learning, striving, aiming, going forward and living your life to its fullest. When you do this, most things will work for you most of the time.

Best wishes to you,
Glenn Harrold

How the CD works

The CD is completely safe, very effective and comes with a clear set of instructions. There are two tracks on the CD. The first track is a full thirty-minute hypnotherapy session that you can use repeatedly. Track Two is the first of seven short four- to five-minute tracks of hypnotic affirmations relating to each of the 7 steps. So Track Two on the CD relates to Step 1 in the book, Track Three relates to Step 2 and so on. You can dip in and out of these mini tracks whenever you want to focus on a specific area.

You must on no account listen to the CD while driving a vehicle or using heavy machinery. The recordings on this CD will guide you into a state of complete physical and mental relaxation, so it is recommended that you listen while you are lying down in a place where you won't be disturbed. For maximum effect, it is strongly recommended that you listen through headphones.

Don't worry if you fall asleep before you reach the end of the track, as your unconscious mind is very capable of absorbing all the positive suggestions even during light sleep states. For more information on how to use the hypnotherapy CD, please visit the 'Frequently Asked Questions' page on the website www.hypnosisaudio.com

Hypnotherapy CD – content, affirmations and sound effects

There are five stages to the hypnotherapy session on Track One of the CD:

1] The introduction
2] The induction
3] The trance deepening
4] Post-hypnotic suggestions and affirmations
5] The awakening

The first thing you will hear is the introductory music and an explanation of how the CD works. After a few minutes, the music fades and you are left with a pleasant voice and some uniquely created sound effects, which will guide you into a state of complete physical and mental relaxation. Some of the sound effects have been recorded at sixty beats per minute to help synchronise the left and right hemispheres of the brain and create a very receptive learning state. The sounds are also recorded in certain keys and at frequencies that induce positive feelings.

During the hypnotherapy session you will hear echoed affirmations that pan slowly from left to right in your speakers or headphones. This deeply relaxing and unique effect is very hypnotic and helps you to absorb each affirmation deeply. In this receptive and relaxed state you will also be given a number of positive post-hypnotic suggestions to help you achieve your goals.

At the end of the recording, you will be brought back gently to full waking consciousness with a combination of suggestions and music. There are also a number of positive subliminal messages embedded in the fade-out music, which facilitate the overall effect.

The important thing to remember is that although you are being guided, you will always remain in full control of the whole process. If at any time you need to awaken, you just open your eyes and you will be wide-awake.

The affirmations and subliminal suggestions on the CD are as follows:

TRACK ONE – a 33-minute hypnotherapy session

- I feel calm and composed under pressure.
- My inner strength grows stronger all the time.
- I feel creative and inspired.
- I live life with courage and confidence.
- I love and respect myself.

The following tracks numbered two to eight on the CD are seven short tracks of hypnotic affirmations relating to each of the 7 steps.

TRACK TWO – 5 minutes, 25 seconds

Affirmations for Step 1 – *De-stress and control your stress levels*

- I feel calm and composed under pressure.
- My nerves grow stronger and steadier.
- I have a positive outlook on life.
- My inner strength grows stronger all the time.

TRACK THREE – 4 minutes, 57 seconds

Affirmations for Step 2 – *De-stress your finances and overcome work stress*

- I release any negative feeling towards money and success.
- I am always in the right place at the right time.
- Abundance flows freely and naturally to me.
- All of my needs are constantly met.
- I deserve to be wealthy and abundant.

TRACK FOUR – 4 minutes, 50 seconds

Affirmations for Step 3 – *De-stress your home environment*

- I have a positive and happy home environment.
- I express my talents in many different ways.
- I feel creative and inspired.
- I have complete faith in myself now.
- I live my life to the full.

TRACK FIVE – 5 minutes, 17 seconds

Affirmations for Step 4 – *De-stress your relationships*

- I am compassionate and understanding.
- I am big-hearted and loving.
- I love to develop harmonious relationships.
- I attract positive people into my life.
- I give and receive love easily.

TRACK SIX – 5 minutes, 42 seconds

Affirmations for Step 5 – *De-stress your health*

- I love being healthy.
- I love to exercise and keep fit.
- I feel inspired and motivated now.

- I deserve to be fit and healthy.
- I love maintaining my fitness levels.

TRACK SEVEN – 5 minutes, 31 seconds

Affirmations for Step 6 – *De-stress your mind*

- I am at peace with myself and the world around me.
- My memory improves with age.
- I remember and recall information easily.
- My mind is calm and clear.
- I believe in myself.

TRACK EIGHT – 7 minutes, 24 seconds

Affirmations for Step 7 – *De-stress your future*

- I have a positive outlook on life.
- I love new challenges.
- I live my life with courage and confidence.
- I draw opportunities towards me.
- I express myself clearly.
- I love and respect myself.

How long should I use the CD for?

There are no hard and fast rules as to how long the CD should be used for, but here are some guidelines.

The hypnosis CD will work differently for each individual. It is impossible to give an estimated time for use, but after listening a few times you should begin to notice some positive changes. Sometimes the positive changes will be instant and dramatic, or you may experience a gradual, subtle progression into new patterns of behaviour over time. For maximum effect, listen to the CD on a daily basis until you feel you have achieved your aim. However, you can also continue listening even after you reach your goals, as it will continue to help to reinforce everything.

The key to absorbing hypnotic suggestion is compounding. This means that the more you hear the suggestions, the quicker your unconscious mind will get the message. You then respond to the suggestions automatically in your everyday life. If you fall asleep listening to the CD but you still hear the count up to ten at the end of the track, you have probably been in a deep trance throughout. In this state you will still be absorbing all the suggestions on an unconscious level. If you don't hear the count up at the end, you have probably drifted into a deep sleep at some point. In this case, you will absorb the suggestions only to the point where you went into a deeper sleep. If this happens, avoid listening when you are tired.

A brief explanation of what happens under hypnosis

In a typical hypnosis session performed by a therapist, the client will be guided into a relaxed state of mind and body through suggestion techniques. When in a hypnotic trance state, brainwave cycles will actually slow down and then quicken again when coming out of the trance, back to full consciousness. The brain cycle states that define our levels of consciousness are referred to as the beta, alpha, theta and delta states.

The frequency of beta waves ranges from fifteen to forty brainwave cycles per second and is typical of full waking consciousness. The alpha state has a frequency range from nine to fourteen cycles per second. This is achieved through relaxation or light meditation. In this state you are still aware of everything around you but your mind is calm and you feel physically relaxed. You are receptive to suggestions and affirmations in the alpha state. Theta brainwaves are typically between five and eight cycles a second. This is the state you achieve when you are in deeper hypnosis. In this very relaxed theta state, hypnotic suggestion can be given and readily accepted and then acted upon at a later date. Delta is the final brainwave state with a range of one and a half to four cycles per second. When you are asleep, your brain cycles will be at around two to three cycles per second. The deepest hypnotic trance state is called somnambulism, which occurs when you are in or close to the delta state.

I always recall the sequence by thinking of the word BATTED – Beta, Alpha, Theta and Delta. The ideal state for absorbing visualisations, suggestions and affirmations is between the alpha and theta states.

A brief guide to self-hypnosis

The following guide to self-hypnosis has a wide variety of therapeutic applications. In particular, it is very effective in the alleviation of stress and tension, in helping to regulate sleeping patterns and when focusing on goals. Self-hypnosis is the ability to focus your energy whilst in a deeply relaxed state of mind and body. When you are in a trance state you can focus your energy on a specific goal or simply quieten your mind and go into a deep state of mental and physical relaxation.

Creating the right atmosphere

Find a quiet room where you will not be disturbed, preferably a bedroom with no telephone. Dim the lights or turn them off. You may choose to light a candle or burn some aromatherapy oils. Use anything that helps you to create a relaxing atmosphere. Then make yourself as comfortable as possible, either in a chair with a headrest or by lying down on a couch or bed.

Once you get skilled at self-hypnosis you can use it in busy places where there are noises and distractions. With practise you will find it easy to block out distractions and still be able to focus your mind intently.

Preparing yourself

Tell yourself silently or out loud that you are going to practise self-hypnosis. Then tell yourself silently or out loud how long you want to remain in the trance. Fifteen to twenty minutes is fine to begin with. However, after a little practise you may decide to make your session last longer.

The breathing technique

Close your eyes and begin to breathe very slowly and deeply, in through your nose and out through your mouth. At the top of your breath, hold for three seconds and then count to five on every out-breath. As you breathe out, imagine you are breathing away any nervous tension left in your body.

Make sure you breathe from your diaphragm (lower chest area) and not from the upper chest. Watch what happens to your body as you breathe. If you are breathing properly, your stomach will go out as you breathe in and will go in as you breathe out. This can take a little practise if you are unused to diaphragmatic breathing.

You can also say the word relax on every out-breath, if you wish. Continue this breathing pattern ten or more times, or as long as it takes for you to feel completely relaxed.

Clearing your mind

This part of the technique is described on page 139, in the mind-calming and body relaxation technique.

Deepening the trance state

By now you will already be in a light trance state. A good technique to guide yourself deeper into trance is to count down silently from ten to one. Feel every muscle in your body relax more and more with each descending number. Leave about five seconds between each number, or count each number down on every second or third out-breath. To enhance this you can also use visualisation techniques. For example, imagine you are travelling down ten flights in an elevator; or stepping down ten steps into a beautiful garden. Count down with each flight or step, going deeper with each number. Use whatever feels right for you. Don't get hung up on the feeling that you are not deep enough in trance or that nothing is happening. Being in a trance is often very subtle. The more you practise the better you will get and in time, you will begin to know intuitively when you are in a deeper, more receptive state.

Conversely, do not fear going into a deep state of trance, as this takes you to a powerful part of yourself where you can make big changes. Allow yourself to go deep inside your mind and tell yourself you feel safe and secure as you do this. Someone once asked me if they could get stuck in the unconscious state. This cannot possibly happen. You may fall asleep in trance, but you would then wake up in your own time, just as you would from a regular sleep state.

Utilising the trance state

When you reach the deeper trance stage, you can either relax and drift or you can give yourself some positive suggestions or affirmations, the wording of which must have been decided upon before you start. You can also use powerful imagery (see 'The power of imagery', below).

Wording your affirmations correctly

Work on only one goal at a time, usually over a number of sessions. Don't, for example, work on releasing a fear and losing weight in the same session. You can use a number of affirmations in one session but they all must relate to your one chosen goal at this time.

Repeat the affirmations over and over in your head, slowly and positively, using as few words as possible. Be very direct, as though you are giving yourself commands. Sometimes you can create a rhythm with your breathing, saying the affirmation on each out breath, almost like a chant or mantra.

When deciding on the suggestions beforehand, always state them as if they are a reality and in the present. This is very important, as your unconscious mind believes exactly what it is told. For example:

- Do NOT say: 'I want to be calm and composed under pressure.'
- DO say: 'I FEEL calm and composed under pressure.' Or 'I AM always calm and composed under pressure.'

You would use the word FEEL if your predominant sense is kinaesthetic (see page 137).

> You must make any suggestion completely unambiguous and Always Accentuate The Positive.

I tend to use the words 'I love to...' to begin many of my affirmations as love is a powerful word and I have found this type of affirmation seems to have a powerful impact.

Really feel the affirmations as you repeat them, draw them inside you and let every cell in your mind and body resonate with positive feeling and emotion. Imagine every part of you is repeating the affirmations with complete conviction and total belief in what you are stating. Even if it feels a bit odd at first, stay with it, as your unconscious mind believes exactly what it is told. You are creating new positive beliefs that will be accepted by your unconscious exactly as they are, without any analysis. That is why taking time and care to list your affirmations correctly is very important.

Bringing yourself back to full consciousness

When you feel it is time to wake up from the trance, all you need to do is slowly and mentally count up from one to ten. Tell yourself you are becoming more awake with each number. When you reach the number ten, your eyes will open and you will be wide-awake with a feeling of total well-being.

If you practise before going to sleep, you do not need to count up from one to ten. Simply tell yourself before you begin that the trance will turn into a deep, natural sleep from which you will wake up in the morning feeling positive and refreshed.

Please note When you first practise self-hypnosis, do not worry if you don't think much happened or you could not see much in the visualisation. Just the fact that you went somewhere quiet and centred yourself by closing your eyes and relaxing will have benefited you.

You will be surprised at how effective a suggestion can be in even the lightest of trances. The power of the unconscious mind works in a very subtle way. The most important thing to remember is to enjoy the process and to have faith, because the more you practise the better you become!

Further resources

Further reading

Steve Biddulph, *Raising Boys: Why Boys Are Different – And How to Help Them Become Happy and Well-balanced Men* (HarperCollins, 3 March 2003)

Steve Biddulph and Gisela Preuschoff, *Raising Girls: Why Girls Are Different – And How to Help Them Grow Up Happy and Strong* (Celestial Arts, 7 February 2006)

Dave Elman, *Hypnotherapy* (Westwood Publishing Company, 1984). A classic on hypnosis first published in 1960 and still very relevant.

Masaru Emoto, *Messages from Water* (Hado Publishing, 1 July 2003). A book revealing how water exposed to positive influences produces beautiful, perfectly formed crystals, while water exposed to negativity produces ugly, malformed crystals.

Glenn Harrold, *Create Wealth and Abundance in 8 Simple Steps* (Diviniti Publishing, 2005). A combined book and hypnotherapy CD to help you create financial abundance.

Karen Kingston, *Clear Your Clutter with Feng Shui: Space Clearing Can Change Your Life* (Piatkus Books, 24 September 1998)

Felicity Lawrence, *Not on the Label* (E-Penguin general, 2 July 2004). An eye-opening book on the food industry. A must-read!

Sheila Ostrander and Lynn Schroder, *Superlearning 2000* (Souvenir Press Ltd, 1996). Tips on learning and memory skills.

Jason Vale, *The Juice Master: Turbo-charge Your Life in 14 Days* (HarperCollins, 4 April 2005). Common-sense advice on healthy eating with many valuable tips. Includes an excellent detox plan.

David Waxman, *Hartland's Medical & Dental Hypnosis* (Bailliere Tindall, 1988). A classic in the field of hypnotherapy.

Stuart Wilde, *The Trick To Money is Having Some* (Hay House, 1995). A brilliant book on the metaphysics of creating financial abundance.

Further viewing

Shiva Rea, *Yoga Shakti* (DVD, Gemini Sun, 19 August 2004). A professional DVD for a complete Yoga workout.
What The Bleep Do We Know!? (DVD, Revolver Entertainment, 26 September 2005). Where science and quantum physics meets metaphysics and spirituality.

Further listening

Glenn Harrold, *Complete Relaxation* (CD and Tape, Diviniti Publishing, 1999)
Glenn Harrold, *Lose Weight Now* (CD and Tape, Diviniti Publishing, 1999)
Glenn Harrold, *Create Unlimited Financial Abundance* (CD and Tape, Diviniti Publishing, 1999)
Glenn Harrold, *Unleash Your True Potential* (CD and Tape, Diviniti Publishing, 2002)

Finding a well-qualified hypnotherapist in the UK

When seeking out a hypnotherapist for a one-to-one session, it is advisable to contact a few in your area. The organisation I trained with, the British Society of Clinical Hypnosis, has a register of qualified hynotherapists throughout the UK. The head office is in London and the number is: 020 7486 3939. The website address is: www.bsch.org.uk

The training is of the highest standard, although the quality of individual therapists can vary. I suggest you call a few locally and find someone who you feel comfortable with. Good therapy is all about the dynamics between the therapist and client. Finding a therapist who inspires you and who can get to the root of your problems is the key.

The APHP is also an organisation of professional hypnotherapists – 01702 347691. They are well-qualified therapists who have organised their own group and have hand-picked other therapists to join them. So, on the whole, they should be good. The website address is: www.aphp.co.uk

UK hypnotherapy college courses:

If you are interested in training to become a hypnotherapist, The London College of Clinical Hypnosis is one of the biggest and best in the UK. Their courses are comprehensive and offer in-depth training in the art of hypnotherapy.

The London College of Clinical Hypnosis
27 Gloucester Place
London
W1U 8HU

Telephone: +44 (0)020 7486 3939
Website: www.lcch.co.uk
Email: info@lcch.co.uk

Qualifying via the London College means you are eligible automatically for membership of The British Society of Clinical Hypnosis. The BSCH have centres all over the UK and the organisation ensures that training is of a high standard. The best way to learn and succeed in hypnotherapy is in a classroom setting with comprehensive training.

For an up-to-date list of Glenn Harrold titles

Contact:

Diviniti Publishing Ltd
P.O. Box 313
West Malling
Kent
ME19 5WE

Telephone: +44(0)1732 220373
Fax: +44(0)1732 220374
Email: sales@hypnosisaudio.com
www.hypnosisaudio.com

Glenn Harrold's personal website is at: www.glennharrold.com